# FIVE-STAR
## Basketball Drills

## Revised Edition

**Edited by Howard Garfinkel**

MASTERS PRESS

NTC/Contemporary Publishing Group

**Library of Congress Cataloging-in-Publication Data**

Five-star basketball drills / edited by Howard Garfinkel.—Rev. ed.
p.     cm.
ISBN 0-940279-22-3
1. Basketball—Training.     I. Garfinkel, Howard.
GV885.35.f58     1988
796.32'32—dc19                                                  88-3652
CIP

Cover design by Susan Milanowski

Published by Masters Press
A division of NTC/Contemporary Publishing Group, Inc.
4255 West Touhy Avenue, Lincolnwood (Chicago), Illinois 60646-1975 U.S.A.
Printed in the United States of America
International Standard Book Number: 0-940279-22-3
25    24    23    22    21    20    19    18    17    16    15    14    13    12    11

# DEDICATION

From its very inception, the Five-Star Basketball Camp has been more than a business, more than another camp, more than a place where comraderie and friendship abound. Five-Star has been a family. This family consists of every camper in every league: the 5', 100-pound eighth grader who attends Pitt-4 to the 7' five-plus prospect, the first-year counselor to those like Hubie Brown or Marv Kessler who have coached or lectured for us for more than twenty years! Thus the family has grown by leaps and bounds, and while we pride ourselves on the fantastic success of so many of our campers, counselors, and coaches, we have endured tragic losses of family members who were equally dear and important to us. It is to those who are no longer able to share with us the basketball excitement and progress that we sincerely dedicate this book.

LEN BIAS (University of Maryland and Northwestern High School)

FRED BOYNE (Thomas Jefferson High School, Elizabeth, New Jersey)

ARTURO BROWN (Boston University and Nazareth High School)

CHARLES BROWN (Thomas Jefferson High School, Elizabeth, New Jersey)

JOHN DAVIS (H.D. Woodson High School, Washington, D.C.)

PAUL FRIEDMAN (Princeton University)

BOB LAPIDUS (*Scholastic Coach* Magazine)

SEAN MANNION (Regis High School, New York, New York)

KEITH MOON (University of Evansville)

GEORGE ROBINSON (Gordon Technical High School, Chicago, Illinois)

CHARLES "DOC" TURNER (Long Island University)

FRANK WILLIAMS (Coolidge High School, Washington, D.C.)

# Table of Contents

## Part One:  Conditioning Drills

# Part Two:  Ballhandling/Dribbling Drills

# Part Three:  Passing Drills

# Part Four:  One-on-One Moves

# Part Five:  Shooting Drills

# Part Six:  Rebounding Drills

# Part Seven:  Defense Drills

## Big Man Development Drills

## Basketball Smorgasbord

# KEY TO DIAGRAMS

| | |
|---|---|
| PLAYER | ❶ |
| BASKETBALL | ● |
| PASS  (AND DIRECTION) | – – – – – → |
| DRIBBLE | ∿∿∿∿∿→ |
| SHOT | 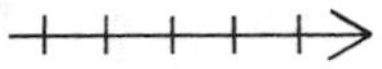 +++++→ |
| SCREEN OR PICK |  ⸺⸺� |
| PLAYER MOVEMENT | ⟶ |
| CONES | ▲ ▲ |
| SLIDE | ⟶ |
| SHUFFLE |  · · · · · · · · ·> |
| IMAGINARY LINE DIVIDING COURT (FOR DRILL PURPOSES) | — · — · — |

# ACKNOWLEDGMENTS

This book could not have been published without the combined efforts of the high school, college, and pro coaches who generously contributed to these drills. Special credit must also be given to Herb Sendek (Providence) and Tom McConnell (Marquette), who provided invaluable assistance in compiling and annotating the drills gleaned from Five-Star Camp's lectures and stations. Our greatest debt of gratitude, however, must be expressed to our twenty-two-year colleague and friend, Bill Aberer (LaSalle Academy), who performed a Herculean task in diagramming and breaking down most of the drills in this book. Also, thanks to Hubie Brown and Marv Kessler for their special flourishes on several drills other than their own, to Tom Konchalski for his valued encouragement, and to Frank Marino for being a legend in his own mind! Special thanks also to the thousands of campers who have attended Five-Star and made it what it is today.

# PREFACE

Over one hundred of the greatest players in the history of the game have made their fame and fortune executing these drills on the way to their dream. And more than five thousand others have "graduated" from Five-Star Camp and entered college on a basketball scholarship. A good part of their hoop education was formulated through these drills at stations, lectures, and individual instruction sessions. In most cases, those who worked the hardest have gone the furthest. Those who are able to see the whole picture grab the brass ring.

That reminds us of the story about the visitor to New York City who approached a stranger and asked, "How do you get to Carnegie Hall?" "Practice, practice, practice," answered the wise city slicker. Our all-pro campers Moses Malone, Jeff Ruland, Michael Jordan, Isiah Thomas, Jim Paxson, Dominique Wilkins, Mark Aguirre, Kelly Tripucka, and Pat Ewing, among others, will be the first ones to tell you that the repetition of most of these drills laid the foundation for their success.

So work hard on these drills within your coach's system, keep a running record of your progress, and become the best player you can be. Where there's a will there's a way. *Five-Star Basketball Drills* could be your way to a four-year college scholarship. Or at least a rewarding high school career.

Yours for better basketball,

*Howard Garfinkel*

*Will Klein*

Howard Garfinkel and Will Klein
Co-directors, Five-Star Basketball Camp

# PART ONE:

# CONDITIONING DRILLS

# Dennis Jackson
*University of Massachusetts*

If this book were a history of the Five-Star Camp, we would tell you why U Mass assistant coach Dennis Jackson is called "The Sandman." Needless to say, there is a connection with putting kids to sleep but this never happens on the court or in Coach Jackson's pre-breakfast workout, which has been an integral part of Five-Star for more than a dozen years. Our head counselor deluxe literally wrote the book on stretching (*A Stretching Program for Athletes*) from which this section is culled. "DJ" came to Five-Star during his reign as assistant head coach at the Junior College of Albany, which preceded a four-year assistantship at Penn, highlighted when the Quakers reached the Final Four in 1979. Prior to entering the coaching and counseling fields, Jackson played four years of quality basketball at Florida A & M.

*Neither rain, nor sleet, etc. can keep Five-Star campers from the swift completion of their appointed rounds with the pre-breakfast workout. Coach Jackson (standing right-center) directs campers on Drill #4 (see page 7).*

Coach Dennis Jackson
University of Massachusetts
Amherst, Massachusetts

# A Stretching Program for Hoopsters

Coach Jackson's stretching program is designed to develop flexibility throughout the entire body, beginning with the upper body and ending with the lower body. For best results, these exercises should be done in sequence. The program is guaranteed to accomplish three things: 1) eliminate soreness, 2) reduce injuries, and 3) increase performance. When the exercises are known from memory, the entire program can be completed in less than ten minutes. This program also can serve as a marvelous pre-game warmup.

Before beginning this stretching program, each player should stand erect, close his eyes, and concentrate on relaxing mentally for ten seconds.

# 1. Waist Stretch Drill

1. Player stands with his feet shoulder width apart.

2. Player places one hand on his hip, raises his opposite arm, and makes a fist with the hand of his raised arm.

3. Player bends to the side at a forty-five degree angle to create a stretching feeling on the opposite side of his waist.

**Points of Emphasis:**

– The drill should be performed several times.

*NITers partake of some individual instruction (Station 13) with Ohio State's first team All-American Dennis Hopson.*

Coach Dennis Jackson
University of Massachusetts
Amherst, Massachusetts

# 2. Back, Hamstring, and Calf Stretch Drill

1. Player stands erect with his feet together and places both hands on his hips (Figure 2-1).

2. Player slowly bends over at the waist without bending his knees and tries to grab his toes firmly (Figure 2-2).

3. Player holds this position for ten seconds, releases, and returns to his original position (Figure 2-3).

**Points of Emphasis:**

- The drill should be repeated two to three times.

*Figure 2-1*

*Figure 2-2*

*Figure 2-3*

Coach Dennis Jackson
University of Massachusetts
Amherst, Massachusetts

# 3. Back and Achilles Tendon Stretch Drill

1. Player stands with his legs about two-and-one-half feet apart (Figure 3–1).

2. Player slowly bends at the waist without bending his knees and places the backs of his wrists on the ground (Figure 3–2).

3. Player holds this position for about ten seconds, releases, and returns to his original position (Figure 3–3).

**Points of Emphasis:**

– The drill should be repeated two to three times.

*Figure 3–1*

*Figure 3–2*

*Figure 3–3*

Coach Dennis Jackson
University of Massachusetts
Amherst, Massachusetts

# 4. Knee, Thigh, and Ligament Stretch Drill

1. Player stands with his feet about two-and-one-half feet apart.

2. Player squats so that his elbows rest on his thighs for balance.

3. Player holds this position for about thirty seconds and then begins to shift his weight slowly from left to right and back again, staying in each squat position for thirty seconds.

**Points of Emphasis:**

– The drill should be repeated two times.

*Oklahoma's All-American, Tim McAlister, displays a perfect release at a shooting station.*

**Coach Dennis Jackson**
**University of Massachusetts**
**Amherst, Massachusetts**

# 5. Groin, Achilles Tendon, and Hamstring Stretch Drill

1. Player stands with his feet about three feet apart.

2. Player shifts his weight downward by bending one knee and squatting on this leg. The opposite leg should be fully extended, with the toes pointing toward the ceiling and the heel of the foot placed on the ground.

3. Player slowly puts pressure on the extended leg and buttocks by pushing downward. The opposite foot should be flat on the ground.

4. Player holds this position for fifteen seconds.

5. Player performs steps 1–4, switching legs.

**Points of Emphasis:**

– The drill should be repeated two to three times.

*Figure 5–1*

**Coach Dennis Jackson**
**University of Massachusetts**
**Amherst, Massachusetts**

# 6. Groin, Hamstring, and Calf Stretch Drill

1. Player stands with his legs spread apart as far as he can withstand the stress. He holds his arms at his sides for balance.

2. Player changes the position of his legs so that he is able to stretch either leg out.

3. Player stretches his left leg out with the left toe and heel pointing upward.

4. Player holds this position for fifteen seconds.

5. Player repeats steps 1 4, this time stretching his right leg.

**Points of Emphasis:**

– The drill should be repeated two to three times.

*Billy Burke, former head coach of Loyola in Baltimore and now a successful Wall Street stockbroker, shows a blue-chip move to Mackin High School player (later Duke University All-American) Johnny Dawkins.*

**Coach Dennis Jackson**
**University of Massachusetts**
**Amherst, Massachusetts**

# 7. Groin Stretch Drill

1. Player sits on the floor and brings his legs and feet inward toward his body, until the soles of his feet are flat together (Figure 7–1).

2. Player holds his ankles and places his elbows on the inner part of his knees.

3. Player grips his ankles firmly and pushes down with his elbows so that he feels the stress in his groin area (Figure 7–2).

4. Player holds this position for ten seconds.

*Figure 7–1*

**Points of Emphasis:**

– The drill should be repeated two to three times.

*Figure 7–2*

Coach Dennis Jackson
University of Massachusetts
Amherst, Massachusetts

# 8. Knee and Ligament Stretch Drill

1. Player squats down and places his hands on his knees.

2. Player brings his legs and knees together, stands halfway up, and slowly moves his knees in a 360 degree circular motion.

3. After he has rotated his knees a couple of times, player bends forward and pushes his knees backward so they become locked.

**Points of Emphasis:**

– The drill should be repeated two to three times.

*There's more to Dennis Jackson than just stretching. Here the U Mass assistant closes a Honesdale, PA session with a stemwinding lecture that drew sustained applause.*

Coach Dennis Jackson
University of Massachusetts
Amherst, Massachusetts

# 9. Groin and Leg Stretch Drill

1. Player stands and lifts one leg straight up in front of him so that it is parallel to the ground.

2. Player holds this position for ten seconds.

3. Player repeats steps 1–2 using his other leg.

**Points of Emphasis:**

– The drill should be repeated two to three times.

– The player should keep in mind that balance is very vital to proper stretching.

*Connie Hawkins, guest clinician, at Station 13. He is one of the many unannounced stars who make surprise appearances at Robert Morris College. The camper being "palmed" by Hawk's huge hand is Garde Thompson, University of Michigan's three-point champion in the 1986–1987 season, then a rising high school star.*

Coach Dennis Jackson
University of Massachusetts
Amherst, Massachusetts

# 10. Body Stretch Drill

1.  Player stands erect and cups his hands together in front of him.

2.  Player turns his palms out and raises his arms above his head.

3.  In one motion, player stretches by standing on his toes and trying to touch the ceiling.

4.  Player holds this position for ten seconds.

**Points of Emphasis:**

– The drill should be repeated two to three times.

*Lefty Dreisell, former University of Maryland coach and currently a successful TV color commentator, works on a drill with a Five-Star hoopster.*

# Bill Donlon
*Northwestern University*

Veteran drillmaster Bill Donlon, who cut his eyeteeth at Maria Regina (Long Island), Methuen High School (Massachusetts) and Providence College, is one of the hardest-working assistant coaches in America. His footwork specialty drills, timed to the quick in a twenty-minute period, remain a mainstay of Five-Star Camp's morning stations. The energized Donlon brings his special brand of intensity to famed Station 13, an optional individual instruction clinic held daily in the afternoon where usually the best come to get better.

*Bill Donlon, assistant coach at Northwestern University, demonstrates footwork in a morning session.*

Coach Bill Donlon
Northwestern University
Evanston, Illinois

# The Science of Footwork

Coach Donlon insists that the game of basketball demands explosive and lightning-quick movements, as well as deliberate movement of the ball and player. But the most important thing is footwork. If the feet and hands are not working effectively, you cannot play! Shooting, playing defense, driving, pivoting, moving without the ball, and rebounding are movements in which correct footwork is essential to complete the play. Drills used to develop correct footwork can be mastered in a minimum amount of time, as long as they are done with maximum effort on an everyday basis. The more time you spend practicing these drills, the better player you will be—it's as simple as that.

# 11. Jumping Drill

1. Player places his feet together and jumps on the balls of his feet, moving from left to right.

2. Player continues jumping in this manner for thirty seconds.

*Figure 11-1*

Coach Bill Donlon
Northwestern University
Evanston, Illinois

# 12. Toe Touch Drill

1. Player stands with his feet apart, jumps upward, and touches his toes with his finger pads as he jumps.

2. Player continues in this manner for thirty seconds.

# 13. Heel Touch Drill

1. Player stands with his feet apart, jumps upward, and touches his heels with his finger pads as he jumps.

2. Player continues in this manner for thirty seconds.

# 14. Heel and Toe Touch Drill

1. Player stands with his feet apart, jumps upward, and alternates touching his toes and his heels with his finger pads as he jumps.

2. Player continues in this manner for thirty seconds.

Coach Bill Donlon
Northwestern University
Evanston, Illinois

# 15. Slide Drill

1. Player stands midway between two imaginary lines twenty feet or more apart.

2. Player assumes a defensive position with his knees bent, head up, and arms out.

3. Player slides back and forth and touches the imaginary lines with his feet, making sure that his feet do not touch each other as he slides.

4. Player continues the drill for one minute.

*No one works harder at Bill Donlon's famed footwork station than the coach himself.*

Coach Bill Donlon
Northwestern University
Evanston, Illinois

# 16. Jump Stop Drill

**Preparation:** Player stands at half court.

1. Player runs and jump stops with his feet parallel to each other, knees bent, head and eyes up, and hands extended out. Player must maintain good body balance with his weight evenly distributed between both feet.

2. Player continues this movement until he reaches the baseline.

3. Player makes a total of three round trips.

# 17. Reverse Pivot Drill

**Preparation:** Player stands at half court.

1. Player runs, jump stops, and executes a reverse pivot, lifting up his heels and pivoting on the balls of his feet.

2. Player continues this movement until he reaches the baseline.

3. Player makes a total of three round trips.

*Mike Fratello's fan club meets following his August 1987 Honesdale lecture.*

Coach Bill Donlon
Northwestern University
Evanston, Illinois

# 18. Back-Door Move Drill

**Preparation:**    Player stands at the baseline.

1.  Player runs to the foul line extended area.

2.  Player plants his outside foot and shows his outside hand.

3.  Player stays low to the ground, pushes off his inside foot while showing his inside hand, and looks for a pass or layup.

**Points of Emphasis:**

– This drill is designed to give players the opportunity to practice the back-door move.

# 19. V Cut Footwork Drill

**Preparation:** Player stands at the sideline area extended from the box.

1.  Player drives hard to the box and plants his outside foot.

2.  Player pushes off his inside foot at a forty-five degree angle, staying low as he drives hard off his foot. He extends his outside hand as if to look for a pass.

**Points of Emphasis:**

– This drill is designed to give players the opportunity to practice the V cut.

## Bill Norton
*Brother Rice High School*

Classic speaker, classic coach!  Certainly one of the best ever to come Five-Star's way.  He developed such Brother Rice talent as  Tim  Andree  (Notre Dame),  John Shasky (Minnesota), Paul Jokisch (super Michigan tight end and part-time hoopster), and Brian Brennan (BC and now Cleveland Brown split end).  He opted for a Michigan State assistantship in 1981 and is presently teaching his heart out at Brother Rice in Birmingham, Michigan.

*Dick Paparo (pointing) and Fred Baraket instruct "campers" at the latter's Officiating School at Radford.  Paparo is a potential "Hall of Fame" referee, while Barakat is Assistant Commissioner of the ACC.*

Coach Bill Norton
Brother Rice High School
Birmingham, Michigan

# The Five-Star Jumping Program

Jumping the way Julius Erving did is a God-given talent. It cannot be acquired by practice and it cannot be taught. However, you can jump a few inches higher and increase your stamina by judicious use of jumping drills. Tips on the offensive board are made by the player who can get up high on the third and fourth consecutive jumps. Fourth-quarter jump shots should feel the same as second-quarter jump shots.

The entire jumping program should take no longer than twenty minutes and should be done every other day. Rules for the program are: 1) jump as high as you can every jump; 2) do not bend at the knees; and 3) rest no longer than fifteen seconds between a series.

# 20. One-Leg Jump

1. Player jumps ten times on his right leg and rests.

2. Player jumps ten times on his left leg and rests.

3. Player jumps thirty times on his right leg and rests.

4. Player jumps thirty times on his left leg and rests.

Points of Emphasis:

- Player should repeat the drill ten times and should then complete three sets of ten repetitions.

# 21. Kangaroo Jump

1. Player takes one step with his right leg, jumps, and comes down using his right leg only.

2. While his right leg is on the floor, player steps with his left leg and jumps, coming down on his left leg only.

Points of Emphasis:

- The drill should be repeated ten times, and the player should complete three sets of ten repetitions.

- This jump series contains the same motions used in shooting layups.

- The player should take no extra steps while performing this drill.

**Coach Bill Norton**
**Brother Rice High School**
**Birmingham, Michigan**

# 22. Step-Over Jump

1. Player moves toward his right, stepping over with his left leg.

2. Player brings his feet together and jumps.

3. As he hits the floor, player begins to move to the left, stepping over with his right leg.

4. Player brings his feet together and jumps.

5. Player zigzags the court as he continues in this fashion.

**Points of Emphasis:**

– Player should repeat the drill ten times and should then complete three sets of ten repetitions.

– This jump series is the same one used in shooting the jump shot off the move.

– The player must make sure he squares up each time he jumps.

# 23. Power Move Jump

1. Player faces the backboard and stands one foot away from it. Player jumps with both feet and touches the backboard with both hands.

2. After he hits the floor, player sidesteps with his inside leg to the other side of the rim.

3. Player brings his legs together and jumps from the other side of the rim.

**Points of Emphasis:**

– The drill should be repeated ten times. The player should then complete three sets of ten repetitions.

# Jerry Wainwright
*Wake Forest University*

Jerry Wainwright is to the impromptu speech what Wayne Gretzky is to ice. Give the man a topic—any topic—and fifteen minutes to prepare and out comes an hour plus of solid fundamentals (if it's basketball), pure common sense (if it's life or academics), or assorted goodies like attitude, big men (tinged with humorous sarcasm), and his latest love, weight training. Adhering to a long-standing Five-Star policy of making weight training and/or Universal training strictly optional, Coach Wainwright implemented manual resistance with a heavy dosage of the jump rope at morning stations. It's a hit. The former two-time Illinois high school Coach of the Year (Highland Park) and current Wake Forest assistant breaks it all down for you on the last of our conditioning drills.

*ACC "Rookie of the Year" J. R. Reid learns post-up technique from a familiar figure, his high school coach Dick Ponti. The feeder is former St. Joe's All-American "Boo" Williams, president of the renowned Boo Williams Summer League in Hampton, Virginia.*

Coach Jerry Wainwright
Wake Forest University
Winston-Salem, North Carolina

# Manual Resistance Training

Manual resistance training is a very effective way to work out. It is utilized a great deal in our in-season program because it is fast, efficient, and does not require equipment.

The following guidelines should be observed when performing manual resistance exercises. It is important to have good communication between the performer and the spotter. The performer must not rest at all during the exercise and must keep his working muscles tense at all times. The performer should take about two seconds to perform the positive portion of the lift and four seconds to perform the negative portion of the lift. The spotter must keep pressure on the performer at all times, but he should apply more resistance during the negative portion of the exercise.

Each person should perform ten to twelve repetitions. By the end of the last repetition, the performer should feel a lot of muscle fatigue in his working muscles.

# 24. Manual Push-Ups Drill

1. Performer presses evenly with his chest as he performs a push-up with his toes touching the floor. If he cannot do this, he should try the push-up with his knees on the floor.

2. Spotter places hands on performer's shoulders and provides resistance by pushing down on both the positive and negative portions of the exercise.

*Figure 24-1*

*Figure 24-2*

**Coach Jerry Wainwright**
**Wake Forest University**
**Winston-Salem, North Carolina**

# 25. Flies Drill (Chest)

1. Performer lies on his back on a bench with his arms out, elbows slightly bent, and palms up. He pulls up with his chest until his hands are together, and he resists until his hands are below his chest.

2. Spotter places his hands on the top (inside) of performer's wrists and offers resistance on both positive and negative portions of the exercise.

*Figure 25–1*

Coach Jerry Wainwright
Wake Forest University
Winston-Salem, North Carolina

# 26. Lateral Raise Drill (Shoulders)

1. Performer stands erect with his head up and his arms at his sides. He lifts his arms to his sides, keeping them straight with his palms down, until his hands are above his shoulders. Spotter faces the performer and places his hands on top of the performer's wrists. He gives resistance on the positive and negative portions of the exercise.

2. Performer resists to his original position on the negative movement.

# 27. Front Raise Drill (Shoulders)

1. Performer stands erect with his head up and his arms at his sides, with his palms facing back. Spotter faces the performer and places his hands on top of the performer's wrists.

2. Performer lifts his arms in front of him, keeping them straight, until his hands are above his shoulders.

3. Performer resists to his original position on the negative movement. Spotter gives resistance on both the positive and negative portions of the exercise.

Coach Jerry Wainwright
Wake Forest University
Winston-Salem, North Carolina

# 28. Military Press Drill (Shoulders)

1. Performer sits upright, bends his arms, and holds his hands with his palms facing forward. Spotter stands behind the performer and places his palms on the performer's palms.

2. Performer pushes against the spotter's resistance to full extension of his arms.

3. Performer resists to his original position on the negative movement. Spotter uses vertical resistance on the positive and negative portions of the exercise.

# 29. Curl Drill (Arms)

1. Performer stands erect with his chest out and his elbows in. He grips a towel by one end with his palms up, while the spotter faces him, holding the other end of the towel. Spotter gives resistance on the positive and negative portions of the movement.

2. Performer pulls against the resistance to his chest, and he holds against the resistance to his original position.

Coach Jerry Wainwright
Wake Forest University
Winston-Salem, North Carolina

# 30. Tricep Extension Drill (Arms)

1. Performer stands erect and grips one end of a towel hand-over-hand, holding it above his head with his elbows facing forward. The spotter stands behind the performer, grasping the other end of the towel. The spotter pulls the towel down to full flexion and gives resistance on the upward pull.

2. Performer resists against the down pull and then pulls to full extension against the resistance.

*Jerry Wainright (left), assistant coach at Wake Forest University, demonstrates the "Tricep Extension Drill."*

Coach Jerry Wainwright
Wake Forest University
Winston-Salem, North Carolina

# 31. Manual Sit-Ups Drill (Trunk)

1. Performer lies on his back with his legs outstretched and holds the spotter's ankles. Keeping his back flat, the performer raises his legs, bending his knees in a ninety degree angle (Figure 31–1).

2. Spotter stands at the performer's head. He places his hands on the performer's knees and pushes the performer's legs to the ground (Figure 31–2).

3. Performer uses his stomach muscles to resist the spotter's downward push.

*Figure 31–1*

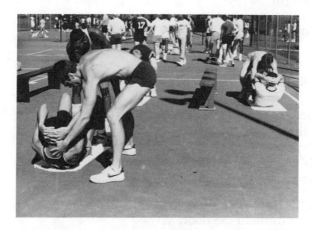

*Figure 31-2*

## Drill 31:  Alternate Manual Resistance Position

*Figure 31-3*

*Figure 31-4*

**Coach Jerry Wainwright**
**Wake Forest University**
**Winston-Salem, North Carolina**

# 32. Back Extension Drill (Trunk)

1. Performer lies face down on a bench with his waist at the edge of the bench and his trunk extending off the bench. The spotter holds the performer's legs firmly against the bench.

2. Performer places his hands behind his head and lowers his trunk to the floor.

3. Performer raises his trunk back to the level of the bench.

# 33. Reverse Dips Drill (Triceps)

1. Performer places his hands, fingers out, with his arms a shoulder width apart, on the bench, with his back to the bench. He moves his body down so that his legs are stretched out straight in front of him with his heels touching the floor. Keeping his back straight, he dips down as far as possible, holds for a count, then pushes up to his original position.

2. Spotter stands above the performer, places his hands on the performer's shoulders, and offers resistance on the positive and negative portions of the exercise.

Jerry Wainwright
Wake Forest University
Winston-Salem, North Carolina

# Basketball Jump Rope Conditioning Program

I believe jumping rope is the best overall athletic conditioner. It is very beneficial to basketball players in that it aids greatly in their development of agility, hand-foot coordination, rhythm, and balance.

A jump rope program improves physical condition and develops strength, endurance, and stamina in the legs, which is so vital to the complete basketball player. The forearm, arm, and chest muscles are also greatly affected by jumping rope.

The greatest muscular involvement and conditioning are possible with the use of a weighted rope. Five-Star has been using the Ultra-Rope® (made by Garney, Incorporated of Grand Rapids, Michigan) exclusively since the 1987 summer camping season. In our opinion, it is the finest weighted rope available.

## Measuring the Rope

The length of the rope is important and varies according to each individual's height. To determine rope length, the player should stand in the middle of the loop of the rope with his feet together and stretch the ends of the rope to his armpits.

A weighted rope, however, requires a shorter length. Using the same technique, the handles of a weighted rope should stretch to just under the player's chest.

## Turning the Rope

When turning the rope, the upper arms are held close to the body. The forearms are held down and out at a forty-five degree angle with the hands eight to ten inches from the hips. The hands and wrists should do most of the work in turning the rope, and should circumscribe a circle of six to eight inches in diameter. The arm movement should be cut down as much as possible.

To start the rope in motion, the player places the loop of the rope behind his heels with his arms extended out in front. He brings his hands down and back for the first turn of the rope. He swings the rope over his head and then under both his feet. The jump should be just high enough for the rope to pass under his feet.

## Terminology for the Jump Rope Program

1. **Single Bounce:** The player bounces only once to each turn of the rope, with both feet together.

2. **Heel-Toe:** The player bounces once to each turn of the rope, alternating his right and left feet so that the heel and toe of opposite feet make contact with the ground at the same time.

3. **Single Speed Bounce:** The player performs single bounces at a rapid pace.

4. **One Foot Single Bounce:** The player bounces once to each turn of the rope, using only one foot at a time, alternating between his right and left feet. He counts and jumps once with his right foot and once with his left foot, then he counts and jumps twice with his right foot and twice with his left foot. The player continues this method of counting up to ten with each foot.

5. **Spread:** The player moves his feet forward and backward alternately: the right foot forward and the left foot back on the first turn of the rope, and the left foot forward and the right foot back on the second turn of the rope.

6. **Straddle:** The player starts with his feet together on the one count or the first turn. He spreads his feet apart sideways six to eight inches on the two count or the second turn, and he places his feet together on the three count or the third turn.

7. **Straddle X:** The player uses a single bounce on the first turn. On the second turn he crosses the right leg over the left leg, then he uncrosses his legs. On the third turn he crosses the left leg over the right leg.

8. **Crossover:** The player bounces with his feet together on the first turn and on the second turn he crosses his arms at the elbows on the downward swing of the rope, jumping through the loop of the rope formed in front of his body. The player uncrosses his arms on the next downward swing of the rope. The crisscrossings are done with a bounce in between the crisscrosses, if so desired, and with the right and left arms alternating as the top arm of the crisscrosses.

9. **Double Jump:** The player makes a single bounce with his feet together while making two turns of the rope. He bends at the waist and speeds up the rope with wrist rotation.

10. **Speed Single:** The player makes a single bounce with one turn of the rope done at a fast pace.

11. **Alternate Jump:** The player runs in place while hitting one fast bounce for every turn of the rope. He lands on the balls of his feet and flexes his lower leg to form a ninety degree angle with the back of his thigh. He may run in place with his knees up or down. Running with the knees up develops the quadriceps and running with the knees down works the hamstring muscles.

12. **Jump through the Rope:** The player doubles the jump rope and holds it taut at arm's length, with his arms shoulder width apart. The player jumps forward through the rope, using a kangaroo jump (bringing his knees up to his chest). There should be no rests or pauses between jumps.

13. **Triple Turn:** The player bounces high once and tries to turn the rope three times before the second bounce. He should concentrate on developing a higher jump and more rapid wrist action.

14. **Jump Square:** The player jumps in a pattern that circumscribes a square.

15. **Front and Back:** The player bounces with his feet together, alternating jumping forward and backward. He should concentrate on swinging his hips forward and backward as well.

16. **Side to Side:**  The player bounces with his feet together and jumps from side to side.  Again, he should concentrate on swinging his hips.

17. **Two Right, Two Left:**  The player bounces once to each turn of the rope, twice on his right foot, then twice on his left foot.  He continues this pattern and constantly tries to increase his speed.

18. **Hula Hoop:**  The player bounces through the rope on the first turn with his feet together.  When the bounce is completed, he brings his hands together and swings the rope on the right side of his body as he bounces again.  He moves his hands apart at the top of the swing and again bounces through the rope with his feet together.  When this bounce is completed, he brings his hands together and swings the rope on the left  side of his body  as  he  bounces  again.  He  continues this pattern as he builds speed and agility.

*Don Matthews, West Florence (South Carolina) High School, gets into the swing of the jumping program.*

# JUMP ROPE ROUTINES

Below are two possible jump rope routines, one based on ten repetitions and the other based on twenty repetitions. Players should also feel free to develop their own routines. It is important to remember that jumping rope should become part of a daily training regimen used throughout the year. A good program utilizes a five- to ten-minute segment during the season and a ten- to twenty-minute routine in the off-season.

| TYPE OF JUMP | ROUTINE ONE | ROUTINE TWO |
|---|---|---|
| Single Bounce | 10 reps | 20 reps |
| Heel-Toe | 10 reps | 20 reps |
| Speed Single Bounce | 10 reps | 20 reps |
| One Foot Single Bounce | 10 right, 10 left | 20 right, 20 left |
| Spread | 10 reps | 20 reps |
| Straddle | 10 reps | 20 reps |
| Straddle X | 10 reps | 20 reps |
| Crossover | 10 reps | 20 reps |
| Double Jump | 10 reps | 20 reps |
| Speed Single | 100 reps | 200 reps |
| Alternate Jump | 100 reps | 200 reps |
| Jump through the Rope | 10 reps | 20 reps |
| Triple Turn | 10 attempts | 20 attempts |
| Jump Square | 10 reps | 20 reps |
| Front and Back | 10 reps | 20 reps |
| Side to Side | 10 reps | 20 reps |
| Two Right, Two Left | 10 reps | 20 reps |
| Hula Hoop | 10 reps | 20 reps |

*Five-Star campers train with the Ultra-Rope® to improve stamina and increase vertical jumping ability.*

# PART TWO:

# BALLHANDLING/DRIBBLING DRILLS

# "Crazy George" Schauer

*Basketball's Greatest Showman*

Maybe we shouldn't blow his cover, but "Crazy George" is crazy like a fox! He has written two books (*Keep the Ball Rolling* and *Basketball Etiquette*), has made 3,000 appearances in eighteen countries and forty-seven states, and has performed in nearly every major arena in the USA. He has 50,000 kids in his fan club, and he has made 4,000,000 people smile, four times as many as his original goal set in 1972—and he's still counting. So is Reebok, for whom he does promotional work.

Schauer joined Minnesota's Golden Gophers as a walk-on in 1971 and when Coach Bill Musselman finally saw him play, he became the "star" of the pre-game warmup. George Schauer holds the all-time Big 10 career scoring record—in reverse—two points! But he's living proof that there is more than one way to skin a cat. He came to Five-Star's June camp in Honesdale in 1974 for a "Ballhandling Wizardry" station, talked us into doing a "show," and the following summer was booked into seventy-five camps. The "6,000,000 Dribble Man" (and he can still pat the rock!) performed at 116 camps during the summer of 1987.

*That's ball spinning, folks!*

"Crazy George" Schauer
Basketball's Greatest Showman

# The Ten Greatest Ballhandling Drills

Fifteen to twenty minutes a day spent on the following ballhandling drills will help anyone improve his ability to handle the ball. The drills should be performed short and hard. Players should strive for increased quickness and intensity to match their level of game play. Whether a player is 5'0" or 7'2" tall, he must have confidence in his ability to hang onto, advance, and protect the ball. The more these drills are practiced, the smoother the performers will become. Then every time a player touches the ball, he will have a lower probability of losing it.

# 34. Slap Ball Drill

1.  Player holds the ball in his left hand and smacks the ball hard with his right hand.

2.  Player holds the ball in his right hand and smacks the ball hard with his left hand.

3.  Player releases the ball and smacks it hard with both hands.

**Points of Emphasis:**

– Players should get in the habit of grabbing the ball hard on a rebound, when receiving a pass, or when going after a loose ball.

*Figure 34–1*

"Crazy George" Schauer
Basketball's Greatest Showman

# 35. Body Circles Drill

1. Player quickly moves the ball clockwise around his neck, waist, both
   ankles, right ankle, and left ankle.

2. As he moves the ball around each body
   part, player hits the ball hard, making
   a smacking sound.

3. Player repeats steps 1-2, this time
   moving the ball counterclockwise.

**Points of Emphasis:**

– Players should feel this drill in their
  arms.

*Figure 35–1*

"Crazy George" Schauer
Basketball's Greatest Showman

# 36. Flip Drill

1. Player bends over with his feet apart and holds the ball with both hands behind his legs.

2. Player flips the ball forward through his legs, reaches forward, and catches the ball in front of his legs with his arms fully extended.

3. Player hikes the ball back through his legs, reaches backward, and catches the ball behind his legs.

4. Player repeats steps 1–3.

**Points of Emphasis:**

– Players should strive for quickness.

– Players should smack the ball hard as they execute this drill.

– This is a great reaction drill for loose balls.

# 37. Flop Drill

1. Player bends over with his feet apart and holds the ball between his legs, with his right hand in front of him and his left hand in back of him.

2. Player switches the positions of his hands quickly so the ball stays in the same place.

3. Player continues to switch the positions of his hands, making sure that the ball stays in the same place as he does so.

**Points of Emphasis:**

– The player should smack the ball hard as he switches the positions of his hands.

*Figure 36–1*

*Figure 37–1*

"Crazy George" Schauer
Basketball's Greatest Showman

# 38. Machine Gun Drill

1. Player sits on the floor with his legs spread apart.

2. Player hits the ball, alternating between his right and left hands, and dribbles the ball between his legs as low and as fast as possible.

**Points of Emphasis:**

– Player should try to make the ball look like a blur as he moves his hands faster than a drumroll.

– This drill is effective in developing the forearm muscles.

*Figure 38–1*

"Crazy George" Schauer
Basketball's Greatest Showman

# 39. Skip Dribble Drill

1. Player stands and moves his legs in a scissors-like fashion, with his toes pointing straight ahead. Player should keep his back straight and should not bend over.

2. Player dribbles the ball through his legs from front to back, from one hand to the other.

3. Player dribbles the ball through his legs from back to front, from one hand to the other.

4. Player should try to complete fifty to one hundred bounces without making a mistake.

Points of Emphasis:

- This is a great coordination drill, especially for big men.

- Players should maintain control of the ball.

- Players should concentrate on quickness.

- Players should not watch the ball as they execute the drill.

*Figure 39–1*

"Crazy George" Schauer
Basketball's Greatest Showman

# 40. Crab Run Drill

1. Player bends over and moves his legs forward and backward in a scissors-like fashion, keeping his toes pointed straight ahead.

2. When his right leg is forward, the player moves the ball behind it and between his legs to his left hand. When his left leg is forward, the player moves the ball behind it and between his legs to his right hand.

3. Player repeats steps 1–2 as he runs up the court, keeping his head up, and making sure to bring the ball behind each of his legs so that if he drops the ball, he will not trip over it.

*Passing the baton: Yale assistant and former BC captain Tim O'Shea was once on the receiving end of instruction as a three-year Five-Star camper. He's now giving back part of what he learned by helping instruct today's campers.*

"Crazy George" Schauer
Basketball's Greatest Showman

# 41. Figure Eight Dribble Drill

1.  Player dribbles the ball in a figure eight fashion, alternating hands. To do so, he begins by standing with his feet apart and leans to the right. He dribbles with his right hand, starting at the outside of his right leg. Then he leans to the left as he dribbles with his left hand. He gives the ball a hard, quick tap from behind when changing hands. The hand that is not dribbling should be between the player's legs ready to make the switch as soon as possible.

2.  Player repeats the drill as he moves forward, dribbling a figure eight behind his legs as he walks. He starts at the outside of his right foot and dribbles behind it, then steps with his left foot and dribbles behind it. He continues up the court in this fashion.

**Points of Emphasis:**

– In step 1, as the player becomes faster, his dribbles should get lower and lower.

– In step 2, the player should keep his hands behind the ball, with his palms up, as he dribbles.

– In step 2, the player should work on coordinating his feet with his hands until he can bend over and almost run down the court. As he becomes faster, he will be able to keep his feet out in front of the ball.

"Crazy George" Schauer
Basketball's Greatest Showman

# 42. Protection Dribble Drill

1. Player zigzags up the court, pretend-
   ing someone is guarding him.

2. Player changes hands as he whirl dribbles and pivots, keeping his knees bent
   on the change of direction.  To protect
   the ball, the player should dribble it at
   his side.

*Overview of a teacher's paradise at Robert Morris College in Coraopolis, Pennsylvannia:*
*sixteen stations all speaking one language.*

**"Crazy George" Schauer**
**Basketball's Greatest Showman**

# 43. Body Control Dribble Drill

1.  Player dribbles forward three bounces. He stops with his knees bent and his feet parallel to each other. He catches the ball in front of him on the final dribble.

2.  Player dribbles backward three bounces. He stops with his knees bent and his feet parallel to each other. He catches the ball in front of him on the final dribble.

3.  Player shuffles to the left as he dribbles three times with his right hand. He stops with his knees bent and his feet parallel to each other. He catches the ball in front of him on the final dribble.

4.  Player shuffles to the right as he dribbles three times with his left hand. He stops with his knees bent and his feet parallel to each other. He catches the ball in front of him on the final dribble.

**Points of Emphasis:**

– When dribbling forward and backward, the player should alternate using his right and left hands.

– Each player should stay under control and strive for greater speed.

– When dribbling, the player should not concentrate on dribbling quickly but rather on stopping quickly with his body under control and his knees bent.

# Rick Pitino
*New York Knicks*

Like it or not, the three-point shot, in one form or another, is here to stay. Rick Pitino likes it! He parlayed the twenty-one-foot line with a 110 percent work ethic and a never-say-die attitude into one of the most astounding NCAA Tourney runs of all time. His 1987 band of overachievers made Pitino the hottest coaching property in the United States. For reaching the Final Four, Pitino was named men's collegiate Coach of the Year by Kodak-NABC, *Sporting News,* and the John Wooden Foundation. The following year, in his first season as head coach of the Knicks, he led them to the playoffs.

Pitino has done everything at Five-Star except cook the meals. He was a prominent camper twenty years ago (NBA high scorer/twenty-five ppg), counselor during his U Mass days, and the youngest stationmaster ever. He won countless titles in camp's NIT, NCAA, and NBA while serving apprenticeships at Hawaii and Syracuse. He manned Station 13 brilliantly as Boston U's boss and New York Knicks assistant and over the years has developed into one of the most profound lecturers in our history. His "Rick Pitino Offensive Improvement Camp" is a smash success at Providence College.

Though at times this drill book will seem like a Rick Pitino anthology, the fact of the matter is we have merely scratched the surface. Our feverish notetakers have recorded stuff ranging from how to lace on your sneakers to how to get your finger-nail on the ball in full-court pressure without losing the fingernail. We have saved many of these tidbits for *Five-Star Basketball Drills II.*

*Rick Pitino (left) with "Boo" Harvey, St. John's University backcourt star. Pitino, then a Knick assistant to Hubie Brown, went on to become head coach of the New York Knicks.*

Coach Rick Pitino
New York Knicks
New York, New York

# 44. Thirty-Five-Second Weak Hand Drill

The main point of Coach Pitino's "Thirty-Five-Second Weak Hand Drill" is that most players are comfortable with the ball when it is in their dominant hand. To be truly effective, a player must be able to handle the ball with equal dexterity and with either hand, moving to the left or the right. A player who is able to move in one direction but not the other is equivalent to a batter in baseball who is able to hit the fast ball but not the curve. Perfect your weak hand and you will hit .400 in any league!

**Preparation:** Player stands at the left box at the far basket.

1. Player dribbles up the court with his left hand (if he is right-handed).

2. When player reaches the opposite basket, he makes a left-handed layup.

3. Player rebounds his own shot and dribbles with his left hand down the court.

4. When player reaches the basket, he makes a left-handed layup.

5. Player continues the drill, moving up and down the court. He tries to make six layups in thirty-five seconds.

**Points of Emphasis:**

- The player should use his weak hand for this drill.

- The player should dribble by pounding the ball into his hands. He should not push the ball way out in front of him and then try to catch up to it.

- The player should always keep his head up.

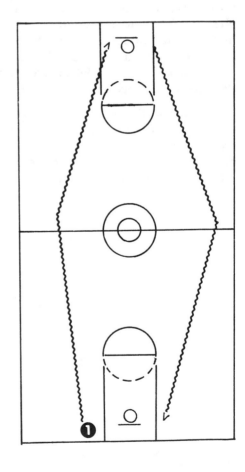

*Figure 44–1*

*An exercise in futility: Rick Pitino (right) shows Garf how to finger the ball for his two-handed set shot. Virginia's Tom Sheehey (second from left) looks on condescendingly, trying to be polite.*

*Rick Pitino practicing what he preaches: about to annihilate an unsuspecting camper at his always-crowded Station 13.*

**Coach Rick Pitino**
**New York Knicks**
**New York, New York**

# 45. Full Court Dribbling and Shooting Drill

In this drill Coach Pitino starts to add to the player's repertoire of dribbling moves by adding a hesitation move to the speed dribble. The drill also aids in the development of three other skills: the layup off a power dribble, the short bank shot off the power dribble, and the corner jump shot off the power dribble. This drill must be executed at game-simulated speeds. To be totally effective on offense, a player must learn to vary speeds with the ball. A pitcher who throws every ball at ninety miles per hour enables the batter to develop a rhythm to his swing. Only by mixing up speeds does a pitcher keep a batter off balance. The hesitation at the hash marks is your change-of-pace pitch.

**Preparation:** Player stands on the baseline on the left side of the court.

1. Player speed dribbles to the first hash mark (position A) and hesitates (Figure 45–1).

2. Player continues his speed dribble to the second hash mark (position B) and hesitates.

3. Player now V cuts with the dribble and goes straight in to the basket for a layup.

4. Player repeats steps 1–3 going the other way on the court, hesitating at position C and position D.

5. Player repeats steps 1–4, except instead of going in for a layup he jump stops on the box for a bank shot.

6. Player repeats steps 1–4, except instead of going in for a layup he circles to the corner for a jump shot.

**Points of Emphasis:**

– The last dribble before the bank shot must be hard to force the shooter to come upright and then go straight up.

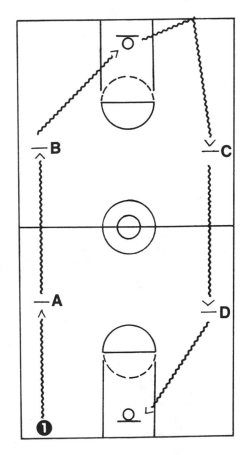

*Figure 45–1*

Coach Rick Pitino
New York Knicks
New York, New York

# 46. Half Court Dribbling and Shooting Drill

In this drill Coach Pitino introduces two new dribble moves: the stutter step dribble and the crossover dribble. The player also works on his weak hand when he alternates sides. This drill also develops another skill: making a layup off a dribble move. Players are encouraged to perform the drill at top speed.

**Preparation:** Player stands on the right side of the court at half court.

1. Player dribbles with his right hand from half court to the right hash mark (position A) and then V cuts with the dribble to the basket for a right-handed layup.

2. Player rebounds his own shot. He then imagines that there is a defender in front of him, and he uses a stutter step dribble with his right hand to avoid the defender.

3. Player dribbles to the half court. When he reaches the half court he begins dribbling with his left hand and keeps his dribble alive.

4. Player repeats steps 1–3, this time using his left hand and beginning on the left side of the court at half court.

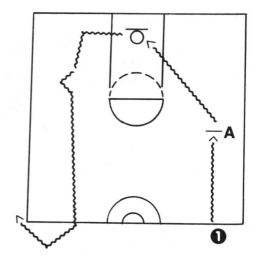

*Figure 46–1*

# PART THREE:

# PASSING DRILLS

# Tony Fiorentino
*Iona College*

Before moving to Iona College as a full-time assistant in 1986, Tony Fiorentino registered 182 wins and only twenty-one losses in his eight-year tenure as head coach at Mt. Vernon (New York) High School. During this stint, he developed the likes of Rodney and Scooter McCray, Ricky Burton (Seton Hall), Curtis Moore (Nebraska), Donald Russell (U Mass), James Gibbs, and Lou Hill (Wichita), and many more collegiate stars. He guided the Knights to two New York Public School state championships.

Tony uses his exceptional teaching and organizational abilities to master Station 13 (see photographs below) and to help coordinate various camp sessions.

**Coach Tony Fiorentino**
**Iona College**
**New Rochelle, New York**

# 47. Rapid-Fire Passing Drill

In this drill Coach Fiorentino intends to develop three basic passes: the two-handed chest pass, the over-the-head outlet pass, and the baseball pass. The drill also helps players 1) to be able to catch hard passes, 2) to deliver the ball quickly, and 3) to develop both wrist strength and eye-hand coordination.

**Preparation:** Player stands about two feet from a wall (or Toss-Back, if available).

1. Player throws a hard chest pass against the wall and continues throwing the ball in a rapid-fire fashion against the wall.

2. As he throws the ball, the player should back up gradually until he stands ten feet away from the wall.

3. Player should continue throwing the ball as he moves back toward the wall until he again stands two feet away from it.

**Points of Emphasis:**

– The player should begin with about twenty-five passes and work up to fifty passes.

– The player can vary the drill by throwing over-the-head or baseball passes.

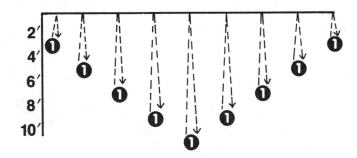

*Figure 47–1*

# Jim Lynam
*Philadelphia 76ers*

Jim Lynam's career spans three decades of greatness. He was St. Joseph's backline leader in the Jack Ramsey NCAA Tourney era of the mid-60s, assistant under Ramsey and head coach of Fairfield and St. Joseph's in the 70s, and head coach of the Clippers and now a 76er assistant in the 80s. No doubt the most memorable of many highlights was the incredible Hawk upset of mighty DePaul, a national TV white-knuckler.

Long before "Kid" Lynam ko'd Mark Aguirre and Co., he was knocking out Five-Star audiences with some of the soundest fundamentals ever taught. He delivers with the directness of a Magic Johnson bounce pass. Someone once asked, "What did Lynam talk about?" The answer was simple: "BASKETBALL!"

*Jim Lynam in action at Radford.*

Coach Jim Lynam
Philadelphia 76ers
Philadelphia, Pennsylvania

# 48. Celtic Drill

Coach Lynam's version of the "Celtic Drill" incorporates many of his teachings, including the outlet pass, the layup at full gallop, the long-distance baseball pass, and the ability to catch on the dead run and put ball to floor for a layup without traveling. The drill is also an excellent tool for building up speed and stamina.

**Preparation:** Player #1 has the ball and stands on the left box. Player #2 stands in the outlet area (top of key extended).

1. Player #1 pitches the ball out to player #2.

2. Player #2 drives wide the full length of the court for a layup.

3. Player #1, after pitching out, sprints to the foul line, turns around, heads back down the court, and looks for a long pass from player #2.

4. After shooting his layup, player #2 gets his own rebound, takes one dribble, and throws a long pass to player #1 who is going toward the hoop.

5. Player #2 sprints to rebound player #1's layup before it hits the floor.

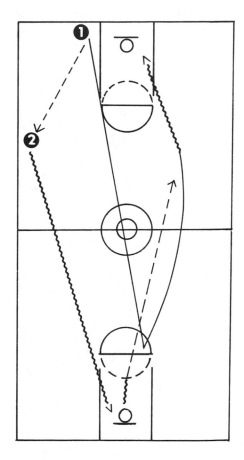

*Figure 48–1*

*The Dodgers came to Three Rivers, but nobody expected a visit from future "Hall of Fame" manager Tom LaSorda.   Following LaSorda's set shooting "exhibition," he delivered a memorable talk to the camp.*

*Guest who came to dinner?    Willis Reed, the heart of the Knicks' championship season of the early '70s, makes a surprise appearance at Station 13.  The "Hall of Fame" center shows some pivot footwork to Billy King (now at Duke) and other aspiring collegians.*

Coach Jim Lynam
Philadelphia 76ers
Philadelphia, Pennsylvania

# 49. Pitch and Fill Drill

Coach Lynam is now developing one of the most basic fundamentals of the fast break—the pitch and fill. Players are drilled in the art of making a proper pitch out pass and immediately filling the lanes wide. The player making the pass must sprint up court and is rewarded for his efforts by receiving a pass for an easy layup. The player receiving the pass is developing the good habit of taking the ball to the middle area. By insisting on the use of the jump stop, this drill insures that the passer at the end of the break is always under control. This drill is a superb pre-season conditioner.

**Preparation:** Player #1 stands under the basket with the ball. Player #2 stands in the outlet area (top of key extended).

1. Player #1 pitches out to player #2.

2. Player #1 sprints widely around player #2 and up the court.

3. Player #2 receives the ball and pushes it at top speed up the middle of the court to the foul line.

4. When player #2 reaches the foul line, he comes to a jump stop and bounce passes the ball to the cutter (player #1).

5. Player #1 shoots a layup.

6. Player #2 follows up for the rebound as player #1 sprints to the outlet area.

7. Players repeat steps 1–6 until ten layup attempts have been made.

**Points of Emphasis:**

– Other passes that can be thrown to the cutter include a pass off the dribble for a layup or an air pass for a baseline jump shot.

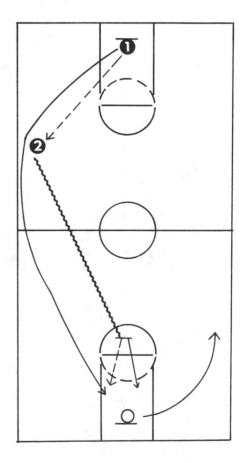

*Figure 49–1*

# Sonny Smith
*Auburn University*

Sonny Smith's reputation for developing the good big man is etched in stone. The blocks of granite are Charles Barkley (76ers), Chuck Person (Pacers' Rookie of the Year) and 6'7'' Jeff Moore, Chris Morris, and Mike Jones. Guards Gerald White and Frank Ford are merely chips off the old block. Sonny was further typed as a purveyor of big-man knowledge when he twice came to Five-Star and delivered valedictorian orations geared drillwise to the "four" and "five" men. The guards and swings were too busy laughing to tune him out.

*Auburn's Sonny Smith leads into the "Bad Pass Drill "(above) and teaches pivot position to Radford campers (below).*

**Coach Sonny Smith**
**Auburn University**
**Auburn, Alabama**

# 50. Bad Pass Drill

Coach Benny Dees, who created miracles at New Orleans in 1986–1987 and has since moved to Wyoming, once told us, "bad hands don't heal." Even Dees would be enamored with Coach Smith's "Bad Pass Drill." Bad hands may not heal but good players catch bad passes. Very few passes in the lane are uncontested. Based on that premise, the player in the paint must be prepared to catch the bad pass and turn it into a bucket or go to the line for two. Coach Smith encourages the bad pass to build confidence and reaction. After working on this drill diligently, we guarantee you will be ready to pull your Willie Mays bit. Utilizing the "overload principle," if you can catch a bad pass, you can certainly catch a good one!

**Preparation:** Player #1 stands on the low box. Player #2 has the ball and stands at the top of the key.

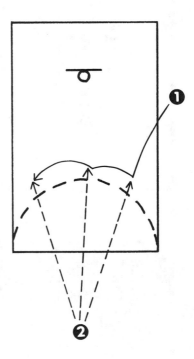

1. Player #1 flashes into the lane.

2. Player #2 throws a bad pass to player #1.

3. Player #1 catches the ball and passes it back to player #2 who immediately throws player #1 another bad pass.

4. Player #1 catches the ball and passes it back to player #2 who again throws a bad pass to player #1.

5. After player #1 catches the bad pass, he turns (pivots) and scores.

**Points of Emphasis:**

– This drill teaches confidence, improves bad hands, and helps hand-eye coordination. It is especially helpful for big, young players.

*Figure 50–1*

# Pat Quigley
*Bishop Loughlin High School*

Though some may not recognize the name, Pat Quigley is one of the best teachers in the game. Well, let's amend that a tad. His CHSAA foes got to know him well over a successful fifteen-year span that resulted in a City Catholic title, a New York State championship, numerous league awards, and the respect of all. And he continues to make a whole bunch of Five-Star friends at famed Station 13 where the level of basketball in this country rises a few notches with his teaching expertise.

*Pat Quigley doing his thing at Honesdale stations . . . making good players better! In the photo at the left, he gears up for the "Monkey in the Middle" drill with Michigan star Rumeal Robinson (center) and a great supporting cast.*

**Coach Pat Quigley**
**Iona College**
**New Rochelle, New York**

# 51. Man-in-the-Middle Drill

Coach Quigley has refined one of the oldest children's games known to man: "Monkey in the Middle." One of his favorite topics is passing, or rather the lost art of it. So what must passing under pressure be? In today's game most passes are contested and the passer is constantly harrassed. In this drill Coach Quigley works on three fundamental passes: the hook pass, the curl pass, and the reverse pivot and curl pass. Since the player passing the ball cannot move, and the defenders are at liberty to do anything legal to challenge the pass, you have got to learn quickly or the "monkeys" won't have any fun.

**Preparation:** Player #1 and player #2 stand at the ends of the foul line. Player #1 has the ball. Player #3 is the defensive player.

1. Player #3 guards player #1 and tries to deflect the pass from player #1 to player #2 (Figure 51-1).

2. Player #1 works on ball fakes and steps through the defense to make the pass. Types of passes to be used include: the hook pass, the curl pass, and the reverse pivot and curl pass (Figure 51-2).

3. When player #2 receives the ball, player #3 hustles over to contest player #2's pass to player #1. Player #2 must wait until player #3 is on him before he attempts a pass.

4. Player #3 stays in the middle and defends both passes until he gets a deflection or until five passes are thrown (Figures 51-3 and 51-4).

5. Players switch positions and repeat the drill.

**Points of Emphasis:**

– All passes should be thrown with one hand (player should alternate using his left and right hands), the off hand being used to protect the ball from the defensive player.

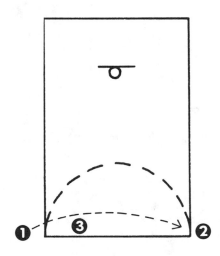

*Figure 51-1*

*Figure 51–2*

*Figure 51–3*

*Figure 51–4*

## Larry Davis
*University of Delaware*

Larry Davis helped develop the likes of Roy Brown (Virginia Tech), Rodney Strickland (DePaul), and Mike Jones (Auburn) during a brief but successful two-year stay at Virginia's Oak Hill Academy. A tireless and creative worker, Coach Davis is an integral part of the Blue Hen resurgence and one of the most popular figures in Delaware basketball as well as at the Five-Star Basketball Camp. His station work is organized, energetic, and resourceful.

*Whether in a crowd or one-on-one, Davis gets the job done.*

Coach Larry Davis
University of Delaware
Wilmington, Delaware

# 52. Passing and Scoring Under Pressure Drill

Recognizing the need for game-simulated drills, Coach Davis has developed a highly competitive practice situation that stresses passing and catching in motion, defensive recovery from the weak side, and putting the ball in the hole while being challenged.

**Preparation:** Player #1 has the ball and stands in the foul lane facing the basket. Player #2 and player #3 stand fifteen feet away on each side of the baseline.

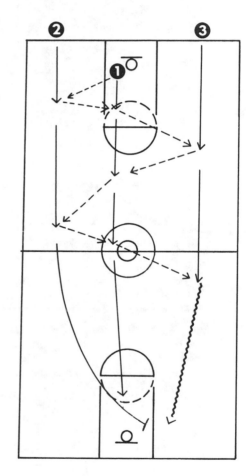

1.  Player #1 throws the ball off the backboard and makes an aggressive rebound.

2.  As soon as player #1 grabs the ball, player #2 and player #3 sprint to the outlet areas.

3.  Player #1 then outlets to either player #2 or player #3.

4.  Player #1, player #2, and player #3 now stay in their lanes and pass the ball up the court by passing the ball from sideline to middle to sideline and back.

5.  The first pass received by either player #2 or player #3 beyond the half court line is taken on the dribble to the basket for a layup.

6.  The player on the opposide side of the player making the layup hustles and contests the layup.

7.  Player #1 rebounds the shot and the drill is repeated.

*Figure 52–1*

*Coach Larry Davis keeping a camper busy in front of a crowd.*

*The world's longest birthday card at Howie Garfinkel's fifty-sixth birthday party on August 1, 1985.*

# Debbie Ryan
*University of Virginia*

When Debbie Ryan took over as Virginia's head women's basketball coach in 1977, national rankings, ACC championships, and NCAA tournaments were far-off aspirations. But after eleven seasons in Charlottesville, she's turned those lofty goals into reality. Ryan's stay at UVA has been highlighted by ten straight winning seasons, six trips to post-season play, national rankings, and ACC regular-season titles in three of the past five years.

1985–1986 marked the most successful season in UVA women's basketball history as Virginia went 26–3, winning the ACC regular-season championship and finishing the season ranked sixth by the Associated Press. That was also the year Ryan was named ACC Coach of the Year—for the third time in four seasons. The next two seasons were anything but let-downs as she went 53–10, for a career mark at Virginia of 220–103, establishing herself as a preeminent women's basketball coach in the NCAA.

*Coach Debbie Ryan gives mid-game instructions to two Cavalier team members.*

Coach Debbie Ryan
University of Virginia
Charlottesville, Virginia

# 53. Team Post Passing Drill

Coach Ryan's drill, which involves the entire team, helps players develop their post passing and outlet passing skills. This drill also emphasizes coordination, movement, timing, and good communication between teammates.

**Preparation:** Players start at the wing and post positions on each side of the key, while the other players line up in two groups at the top of the key (Figure 53–1). The first player in each line has a ball.

1. The first player in each line passes to the wing player.

2. The wing player on each side passes to the post player, using a bounce or lob pass.

3. The post player on each side pivots and throws an outlet pass to the first player in the opposite line.

4. The first player in line moves to the wing, the wing moves to the post, and the post moves to the end of the opposite line.

5. Players should repeat the drill three times, or as directed by the coach.

**Points of Emphasis:**

– When passing to the wing, players should try to pass to the outside of the defender.

– When passing to the post, players should try to get their hands past the defender.

– Players can promote good communication skills by calling out each receiver's name during this drill.

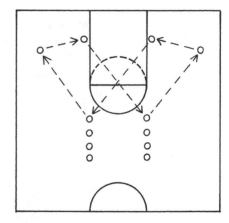

*Figure 53–1*

*Mourning skies!*

# PART FOUR:

# ONE-ON-ONE MOVES

# Tom McConnell
*Marquette University*

Tom McConnell is continuing a Five-Star tradition that we hope never ends: discovering dynamic teachers and coaches with bright, young basketball minds. Our job has been made more difficult by the college presidents who, in their infinite wisdom, eliminated the part-time guy from each Division I and II staff. We hope the NCAA will correct this madness when next they meet! Fortunately, the ex-Davidson backcourt product is now a full-fledged aide after coming over from Wake Forest as the part-timer. Others are not so fortunate. McConnell, who was one of the major notetakers for this book, is rapidly developing into one of the most well-rounded stationmasters in the sport. His perpetual motion style is reminiscent of a younger Rick Pitino. No, we didn't quite rob the cradle to get him.

*The always inventive McConnell remains unbeaten and untied in "Simon Says."*

Coach Tom McConnell
Marquette University
Milwaukee, Wisconsin

# 54. One-on-One Spot Drill

Coach McConnell has developed a very simple yet highly relevant drill to emphasize the one-on-one move. You will work on your jab step series, ball fake moves, head and shoulders fakes, and crossover dribbles, all from various spots on the floor. Today, because of the three-point shot from child's play distance, coaches are stressing solid man-for-man as their primary defense. This means you will have fewer opportunities to receive the ball unattended. The good player must develop his one-on-one game and the only way to do that is with constant practice against another player who is serious about stopping you.

**Preparation:** Player #1 has the ball and stands directly beneath the basket. Player #2 stands between player #1 and the baseline.

1. Player #1 dribbles to any spot on the floor within twenty-two feet of the basket.

2. Player #1 sets the ball down and gets into a defensive stance.

3. Player #2 follows player #1, picks up the ball, and gets into a triple threat position.

4. The two players play one-on-one until player #2 scores or until player #1 stops him. If player #1 fouls player #2, player #2 retains possession of the ball. The offensive player is permitted only three dribbles.

5. Play continues until a player scores eleven points, with each basket counting as one point.

6. The two players reverse positions and repeat steps 1–5.

**Points of Emphasis:**

– Players should take the ball to a different spot each time the drill is performed.

– Players should always square up to the basket and locate the rim to enable them to see the entire floor.

– The offensive player should drive at the defender's front foot.

– The offensive player should utilize both shot fakes and ball fakes to get the defensive player out of his stance.

– The offensive player should occasionally use a six- to eight-inch jab step directly at the defender to keep him off balance.

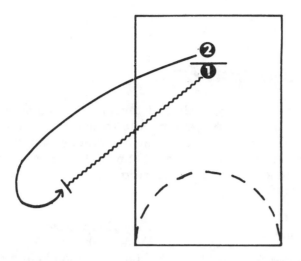

*Figure 54–1*

*Coach McConnell demonstrates paths through his obstacle course.*

**Coach Rick Pitino**
**New York Knicks**
**New York, New York**

# 55. One-on-One Touch Drill

Coach Pitino is a master at creating drills that mirror game situations. His drills are always geared toward making his players work to their maximum under pressure conditions. In this drill the players continually play one-on-one from various spots on the floor while alternating possessions. In Coach Pitino's drills there is always a goal or a time limit on each sequence. This drill is performed until one player has scored a total of nine points.

**Preparation:** Player #1 stands under the basket and player #2 stands in the corner.

1. Player #1 throws a chest pass to player #2.

2. Player #2 catches the ball ready to shoot in an athletic position as player #1 runs at him.

3. Player #1 touches player #2's hip, and the two players then play one-on-one.

4. Play continues until offense scores, defense rebounds, offense turns the ball over or defense steals, or one of the players fouls. If a player scores or gets fouled, he keeps the ball.

5. Players repeat steps 1–4 from positions A through I in Figure 55–1, scoring from a position before moving to the next position.

6. Play continues until a player scores nine points. A basket is worth one point, and if a player fouls he loses a point.

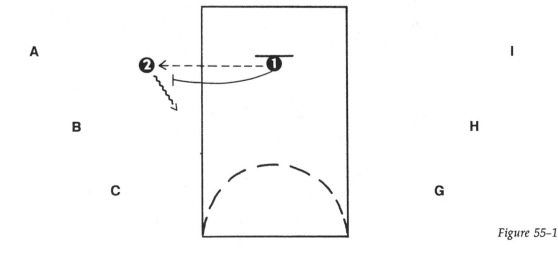

*Figure 55–1*

Coach Rick Pitino
New York Knicks
New York, New York

# 56. One-on-One Dribble Drill

Ever the innovator, in this drill Coach Pitino has modified his "One-on-One Touch Drill" to include another facet of the game. Instead of waiting for the defensive player to touch your hip, you are allowed to start your move as soon as you catch the ball. This forces the offensive player to develop moves off the dribble instead of moves from a stationary position. It also puts more pressure on the defender. Once again, the players have a definite goal—a nine-point game.

**Preparation:** Player #1 has the ball and stands under the basket. Player #2 stands in the corner.

1. Player #1 throws a bounce pass to player #2.

2. Player #2 does not wait for the defender (player #1) to touch him (as in the "One-on-One Touch Drill"). Instead, player #2 dribbles at player #1 and tries to go by him.

3. Player #1 tries to meet player #2 outside the lane and force him laterally.

4. Play continues until offense scores, defense rebounds, offense turns the ball over or defense steals, or one of the players fouls. If a player scores or gets fouled, he keeps the ball.

5. Players repeat steps 1–4 from positions A through I in Figure 55–1, scoring from a position before moving to the next position.

6. Play continues until one player scores nine points. A basket is worth one point, and if a player fouls he loses a point.

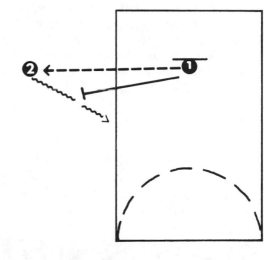

*Figure 56–1*

# Pete Gillen
*Xavier University*

"The Voice" is not as shrill as it once was, say fifteen years ago, but it's still an attention-getter for some, an instrument of high tech learning for others, and a lifesaver for a few (Bob Knight came up hoarse one day at Five-Star and The Voice pinch hit as Knight whispered instructions). The Voice belongs to Pete Gillen, the carrot-topped head coach of Xavier University in Cincinnati, and it sings an aria of hoop lingo that would make Placido Domingo sit up and take notice.

We first heard The Voice booming out at Brooklyn Prep High School and knew we had to have that sound at Five-Star. When he moved to Nazareth High in 1973 he hummed our tune. The Voice has been hitting the high notes ever since. It said hello to Rick Pitino at Hawaii where they were both assistants, greeted Charlie Schmaus at VMI, crooned to Rollie Massimino at Nova, and chanted the Notre Dame fight song for five years for "Digger." He took over a winning program at Xavier in 1985-1986, never missing a beat as he guided the Musketeers to Midwestern City League and Tourney honors (25-5), was named Co-Rookie Coach of the Year, and was ranked eighth nationally on the AP list. But in 1986-1987 he truly belonged at the Met. Despite losing six seniors—including a quartet of starters—Gillen warbled during the regular season, then hit Pavarotti-like high C's at tourney time to bring the house down again. In the NCAAs Xavier upset fourteenth-ranked Missouri and Gillen vocalized nicely against Duke until he hit a sour note late in the second act. CBS's Brent Mussberger said a mouthful when he intoned, "He's in on every play, he's one of the best coaches in America."

With the metabolism of a hummingbird, Gillen has invented and taught stations like "Feeding the Pivot" (a big hit at the MacGregor Clinics) and "Good Hands" (using every ball imaginable except a ping-pong ball), and gets a standing ovation at all his Five-Star lectures.

*Pete Gillen, whose one-on-one moves will keep you busy for weeks, teaches Pitt-1's Development Leaguers proper defensive stance.*

Coach Pete Gillen
Xavier University
Cincinnati, Ohio

# 57. Up-and-Under Move

These four one-on-one moves are part of Coach Gillen's Station 13 routine, and each drill's importance for guards and small forwards is self-explanatory.

**Preparation:** Player #1 has the ball and stands one-half step above the box in the low post area. Player #2 is the defensive player and stands near player #1. Player #2 has the ball.

1. Player #2 throws the ball to player #1.

2. Player #1 catches the ball, making sure his knees are bent.

3. Player #1 turns, pivots on his left foot, squares up, faces the baseline, and makes a violent pump fake, bringing the ball up to his forehead.

4. Player #1 takes one hard dribble with the hand furthest away from player #2 and takes the ball hard to the basket.

5. Player #1 ducks under and goes to the basket. If player #2 stays on the ground, player #1 jumps in the air after his pump fake, squares in the air to the basket, and shoots the ball.

**Points of Emphasis:**

- Player #1 must remember to keep his knees bent until after he makes his pump fake.

- Players should practice this move twenty-five times per day from each side of the court.

**Coach Pete Gillen**
**Xavier University**
**Cincinnati, Ohio**

# 58. Spin-Back Move

**Preparation:** Player #1 stands one-half step above the box. Player #2 stands near player #1 and acts as the defender. Player #2 has the ball.

1. Player #2 throws the ball to player #1.

2. Player #1 catches the ball and takes one dribble toward the middle of the lane.

3. When player #1 feels contact from player #2, player #1 spins back, pivots off his right foot, squares up, and shoots a bank shot. Player #1 dribbles only once and keeps the ball low between his legs.

**Points of Emphasis:**

– Player #1 must remember to get low and have his knees bent.

– This is a move that professional players use often.

– Players should practice this move twenty-five times a day from each side of the court.

*Jim Boeheim, head coach at Syracuse University, teaches passing at Honesdale to Marty Headd, former Syracuse scoring leader.*

Coach Pete Gillen
Xavier University
Cincinnati, Ohio

# 59. The Jim Paxson Move

**Preparation:** Player #1 and player #2 stand to the left of the key. Player #1 is the offensive player and player #2 acts as the defender. Player #1 has the ball.

1. Player #1 drives down the lane with player #2 on his side.

2. Player #1 slows down at the last second as he gets close to the basket.

3. Player #1 lets player #2 get slightly ahead of him.

4. Player #1 comes to a jump stop and then pivots off his foot closest to the foul line (the right) as his feet hit the ground.

5. Player #1 turns and takes a baby hook shot as he comes toward the middle of the lane.

**Points of Emphasis:**

– Players should practice this move twenty-five times a day from each side of the court.

Coach Pete Gillen
Xavier University
Cincinnati, Ohio

# 60. Shake-Dribble Move

**Preparation:** Player #1 stands at mid-court and player #2 stands at the edge of the key. Player #1 has the ball.

1. Player #1 holds the ball low, slightly ahead of him and slightly to his side. He dribbles straight up to player #2, comes to a stop, and continues to dribble the ball.

2. Player #1 shakes his head, shoulders, and body from side to side without moving forward or backward. The purpose of this move is to get the defensive player off balance and back on his heels.

3. Player #1, who has kept his dribble alive for the entire move, explodes to the basket and goes in for a layup. He may keep the ball in his right hand or he may cross over to his left hand.

**Points of Emphasis:**

– Players should practice this move twenty-five times per day from each side of the court.

*A bespectacled Dick Vitale—in pre-ABC network days—mesmerizes Pittsburgh campers. Vitale, then and now, is one of the world's great motivational speakers.*

# Steve Lappas

*Villanova University*

Here's a prediction: Coach Steve Lappas will one day write his own drill book. The former coach of Truman High School, which captured the New York City Public School flag in 1984, is a drill-a-minute wonder who never seems to run out of ideas or energy. Steve's big gamble paid off in May of 1987 when the part-time Villanova coach was moved up to first assistant, the fourth Five-Star resident coach to be hired by Rollie Massimino.

*A fast-break station at Five-Star.*

Coach Steve Lappas
Villanova University
Villanova, Pennsylvania

# 61. V Cut Drill

Here Coach Lappas incorporates one-on-one moves, shooting, and especially foot-work into a terrific drill for the individual player.  It is amazing how many so-called big-timers cannot make a fundamentally sound V cut.  You walk the defender toward the basket at your own speed, push hard off your baseline foot, and explode back toward the ball.  After you pick up the ball, you pivot on your baseline foot into the triple threat position with the ball in your "holster" and your eyes on the rim.  You are now ready to complete the drill according to the instructions.

**Preparation:** Player stands at the position indicated in Figure 61–1.

1. Player places the ball on the floor.

2. Player steps back and makes a V cut to the ball (Figure 61–1).

3. Player picks up the ball, makes an offensive move, and takes a shot.

4. Player gets his own rebound and repeats steps 1–3 from positions A through I in Figure 61–1.

**Points of Emphasis:**

– Players are encouraged to use different offensive moves from different positions on the floor.

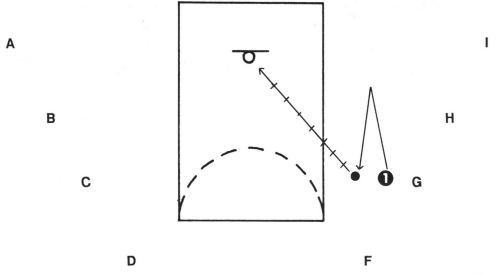

*Figure 61–1*

*"The Garf" poses with legendary Knick forward Bernard King following King's historic lecture in Honesdale.*

## Howie Landa

*Mercer County Community College*

Howie Landa is to junior college coaching what Nobel is to the Peace Prize. This "goodwill ambassador of Juco" raises the level of basketball wherever he goes, and he's been all over the map. Last spring he went to Yugoslavia, a pit stop compared to his clinics in Czechoslovakia, Italy, Israel, and Japan. He's been lecturing faithfully at the Five-Star Camp for years as well as at his own All-Pro Basketball Camp and at men's and women's schools all over the East. Landa's dynamic and innovative speeches are classics of the genre. He also talks from experience, having been a top-flight backcourt player in the Eastern Pro League for years.

The "Landa-Man" has an ongoing coaching career at Mercer (formerly Trenton Junior College) that is nearly unparalleled in Juco annals. He won national titles in 1973–1974 and 1974–1975, was runner-up in 1968 and 1976, and was named Coach of the Year on three different occasions. We vividly remember the "midnight" scrimmages at Trenton, when college coaches like Paul Brandenburg and Dave Pritchett would convene for a little extracurricular recruiting activity. His camp name, All-Pro, was not manufactured by accident. He's had a close association with a bevy of pro stars, Dave Bing and Maurice Lucas in particular, and his name is constantly surfacing for assistant coaching jobs. In 1985 Howie Landa was inducted into the Junior College "Hall of Fame."

*Landa holds court in gorgeous Dedmon Center at Radford University.*

Howie Landa
Mercer County Community College
Trenton, New Jersey

Coach Landa's penchant for detail was never more obvious than in his written description of how to set and cut off screens. Most young players we know—and some older ones, too—screen air. These drills will teach you to "head hunt," and your coach will think you're a genius. Without screens and cuts there is no movement. Without movement there is no game!

# Setting and Cutting off Screens

**Side Screens:** According to the rule book, in setting a blind side screen the offensive player must give three feet; in setting a strong side screen he must not give any distance, as long as neither screen is an illegal "moving screen." The player setting the screen must be stationary when contact is made by the defensive player. If the defensive and offensive players do not make contact with each other, an illegal screen call cannot be made.

**Front and Back Screens:** In front screening the offensive player faces the defensive player, and in back screening the offensive player faces the basket. To execute a front screen, the player should keep his elbows extended four to six inches from his body, with his arms folded in and his hands in loose fists six to ten inches away from his body at chin level. The player should be comfortable, with his body bent and his backside out.

The offensive player can set up the defensive player by walking or running at different speeds. In order to do this, the offensive player comes from the wing and tries to take down the defensive player at least three feet. Out front cutting off a post or wing screen, the offensive player should line himself up in order to be able to cut off the screen. This can be done with a front door (ball side) or back door (away from the ball) screen.

To cut off a side screen from outside, the offensive player sets up the defensive player and comes off the body of the defensive player as closely as possible. As a target for the passer, the offensive player holds his outside hand open at face level with his elbow extended out a full twelve inches. He uses his forearm to pin the defensive player against the screen (block) of his teammate. Moving from right to left, the offensive player uses his right forearm to pin the defensive player, and he keeps his left hand open as he asks for the ball (opposite arms are used if the player moves from left to right).

## Four Ways to Cut off a Screen Directly in Front of a Player:

1. The player plants his left foot equal to the screener. He plants his right foot when the player front screens, and he plants his left foot on the left foot of a back screener. He explodes off his right foot toward the ball for a front door cut.

2. For back door action the player plants his right foot, explodes off his left foot, holds his arms up and his elbow out, pins the defensive player against the screen with his forearm (elbow), and cuts off the screen as closely as possible at the last second.

3. The player runs directly into the screen, plants his right foot in the middle of the defensive player, rolls toward the ball, and hooks the defensive player against the body of the screen, keeping his elbows in the block out position.

4. The player plants his left foot directly in the middle and rolls away from the ball using a block out technique such as rolling toward the basket.

*Famed CBS hoop analyst Billy Packer gives some mike hints to Billy Owens, but Owens does most of his talking on the court: he led Carlisle to four straight Pennsylvania state titles; was named co-MVP of the '88 McDonald's East-West game and co-Player of the Year; and has twice received Five-Star's Outstanding Player Award. Behind Packer and Owens is Five-Star's "Wall of Fame."*

Coach Howie Landa
Mercer County Community College
Trenton, New Jersey

# 62. Screen and Roll Drill

**Preparation:** Player #1 stands at the top of the key on the left side. Player #2 stands in the foul line extended area and player #3 stands at the left elbow. Player #1 has the ball.

1. Player #2 V cuts to the ball as player #1 passes the ball to him and screens away to the opposite side (Figure 62-1).

2. When player #2 receives the ball, player #3 immediately sets a front screen on player #2's imaginary defensive player (Figure 62-2).

3. Player #2 drives his imaginary defensive player off player #3's screen.

4. Player #2 drives off the pick wide in order to set up a possible passing lane.

5. Upon impact, player #3 opens up to the ball and rolls to the basket, giving his target (left) hand as he is going to the basket.

6. Player #2 has three options: 1) he may hit player #3 with a pass going to the hoop, 2) he may hard dribble to the basket for a layup, or 3) he may come to a jump stop on the foul line and make a jump shot.

7. Players rotate positions and repeat the drill.

**Points of Emphasis:**

- In step 3, player #2 should try to brush his shoulders with the screen as he comes off the pick.

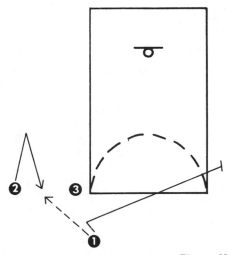

*Figure 62-1*

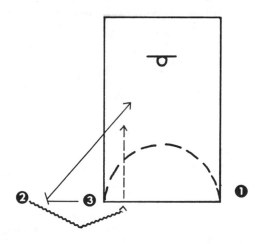

*Figure 62-2*

**Coach Howie Landa**
**Mercer County Community College**
**Trenton, New Jersey**

# 63. Pass and Go Away Drill

**Preparation:** Player #1 stands at the top of the key with the ball. Player #2 and player #3 are positioned at the left and right foul line extended areas.

1. Player #1 dribbles toward player #2 (Figure 63–1).

2. Player #2 V cuts toward the ball.

3. Player #1 passes to player #2 and then screens away for player #3.

4. Player #1 screens an imaginary player but he should be drilled to "head hunt" the defensive player in a game situation.

5. Player #3 V cuts around the screen and toward the basket.

6. After player #3 cuts, player #1 opens up and rolls toward player #2, who has the ball (Figure 63–2).

7. Player #2 has the option of either hitting player #3 cutting to the basket or player #1 rolling back to the ball.

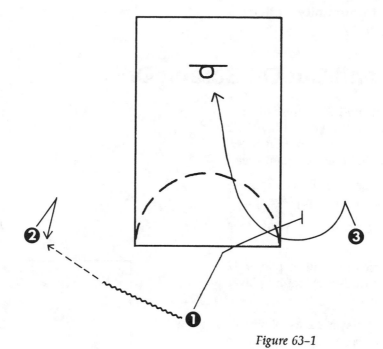

*Figure 63–1*

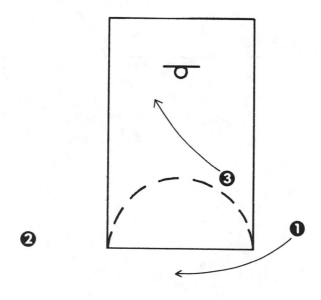

*Figure 63–2*

Coach Howie Landa
Mercer County Community College
Trenton, New Jersey

# 64. Pass and Cut Off Screen Drill

**Preparation:** Player #1 has the ball and stands to the left of the key. Player #2 stands at the left elbow and player #3 stands in the left foul line extended area.

1. Player #3 moves to the elbow, faces the ball, and sets a screen on player #2.

2. Player #3 releases to the wing area (Figure 64–1).

3. Player #1 passes the ball to player #2 and V cuts off the screen set by player #3 on the elbow.

4. Player #2 hits player #1 as player #2 cuts to the hoop for an easy layup (front door, Figure 64–2).

5. Player #1 may also V cut behind the screen set by player #3 on the elbow (back door, Figure 64–3).

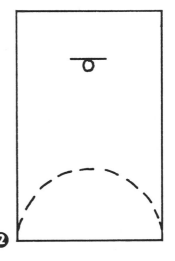

*Figure 64–1*

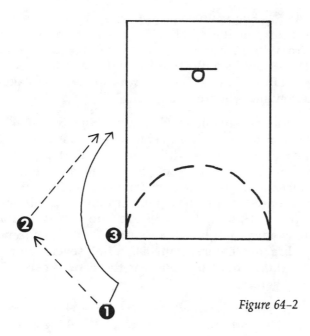

*Figure 64-2*

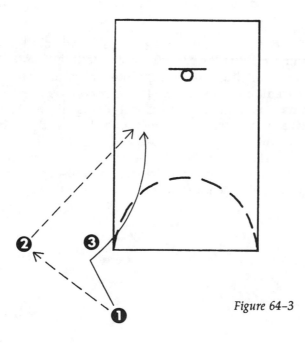

*Figure 64-3*

# Hubie Brown
*CBS-TV*

Hubie Brown is rated the top hoop clinician in America by his peers and is one of the finest teachers in the history of the sport. Like most of the legendary teacher-coaches, Brown emerged from the high school ranks. He played his high school ball at St. Mary's of Elizabeth (New Jersey), was part of a fabled Niagara team in 1953–1955, played service ball in 1957 and 1958, and was an Eastern League hard-noser from 1960–1962 with Hazelton and Allentown.

Brown's first coaching magic was unveiled at Fair Lawn High School when he turned that quiet New Jersey suburban town into an overachiever's paradise. He seemingly breezed through assistant coaching tenures with William and Mary, Duke, and the Milwaukee Bucks. Daily contact with two of the game's all-time best, Kareem Abdul-Jabbar and Oscar Robertson, prepared him for the rigors of the ABA. In 1975 he guided the Kentucky Colonels to the championship and the following year was named head coach of the Atlanta Hawks. He took over the lowest paid and youngest team in pro basketball and steadily built it into a Central Division contender. Then in 1979 the Hawks won forty-six games before losing a thrilling seven-game playoff series to eventual NBA champ Washington. The next year the Hawks copped the division title, winning a coveted fifty games.

The New York Knicks represented the biggest challenge of Hubie's coaching career. He met it head on, and within a short time the Garden was rocking again. The playoff goal was reached in 1982 and credibility was established in 1983 when the Knicks took the championship Celtics to a seventh playoff game. This promising start collapsed under the weight of devastating injuries during the next two-and-one-half years. In 1979 and 1980 Brown was named NBA Coach of the Year by the basketball writers and by CBS-TV, respectively.

Coach Brown's meteoric rise to the top of his profession mirrored his years at Five-Star. In 1966 he brought one-third of the camp's total enrollment from Fair Lawn, and history was in the making. His drills, teaching philosophy, and enthusiasm remain cornerstones of Five-Star tradition. For five years he served as head coach, was one of our first super stationmasters, and each of his lectures is still more of a happening than a speech. His motivational talks to major corporations and the hoop clinics he conducts throughout the country for high school and college coaches are classics of construction, delivery, and knowledge. Coach Brown is presently in the employ of CBS-Sports, where his color commentary on collegiate and NBA basketball has received rave reviews. In 1987 he turned down a solid offer to coach the L.A. Clippers.

**Coach Hubie Brown**
**CBS–TV**

Five-Star Camp encourages its players to use the baby hook when driving in the paint. Sometimes the baby hook cannot be used because the lane is too crowded or players are matched up against bigger opponents, so we teach as an alternative the step-back move. This move allows a player to score in the lane over opponents who may be a foot or so taller.

# 65. Step-Back Move

**Preparation:** The player stands at the top of the key.

1. Player dribbles hard to the right side of the broken circle.

2. Player makes a big step with his lead foot in order to get the defender to extend his stance.

3. Player jumps back as quickly as possible and shoots a quick jump shot.

4. Player repeats the drill from the left side of the court.

**Points of Emphasis:**

– The player's goal should be to perform step 3 as quickly as possible.

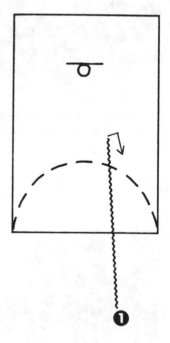

*Figure 65–1*

*Hubie Brown imitates an airplane take-off, which his career did shortly after this Station 13 stint at the old Rosemont site in Honesdale, Pennsylvania.*

# PART FIVE:

# SHOOTING DRILLS

# Al Rhodes
*Warsaw High School*

When Al Rhodes took his lightly regarded and physically underwhelming cast of Warsaw Tigers to the Indiana State Championship in 1984, little did he realize he was acting out a mini version of the movie *Hoosiers*. Though somewhat more compassionate than Gene Hackman, Rhodes's accomplishment was equally compelling. He shocked heavily favored Vincennes preceding Marion's (Edwards and Jones) incredible run of three consecutive state flags. The engineer of that streak was Bill Green (now Indianapolis University), who shattered the legendary Everett Case's record with his fifth state title. Incidentally, one of Rhodes's players in that championship season played a key role in *Hoosiers*. Of course, Steve Hollar was a Five-Star camper!

Rhodes, who doubles as one of the best math teachers anywhere, journeys to Australia in the summer of 1988 to give clinics in an exchange program, breaking a string of six straight years at Five-Star. He guided the U.S. All-Stars to a resounding win over a strong Metro D.C. team in McDonald's 1988 Capital Classic held in Landover, Maryland.

*Jeff Ruland (left) of the Washington Bullets at Station 13 (individual instruction on practice courts in Radford, Virginia).*

Coach Al Rhodes
Warsaw High School
Warsaw, Indiana

# 66. Basketball Golf Drill

Al Rhodes has invented a very simple game in which a single player can practice his shooting under a certain amount of pressure. Shots from spots B, D, and H should be cast from the twenty-one-foot three-point line, since the three-point national high school rule came into effect in the 1987-1988 season. Fore!

**Preparation:** Player stands at position A (Figure 66–1).

1. Player shoots from position A until he makes a shot.

2. Player advances to each position on the court (B–I), remaining at a position until the shot is made, and advancing to the next position after completing the shot.

**Points of Emphasis:**

– All forty-five degree shots must be banked.

– Players should move quickly from position to position.

– Players should try to complete the circuit with fewer than eighteen shots.

– This drill shows each player how good a shooter he is from all areas. It should be used with spot-shooting drills.

– To practice spot shooting, the player should pick five positions on the court and shoot fifty shots from each position.

– A rebounder is helpful for this drill if one is available.

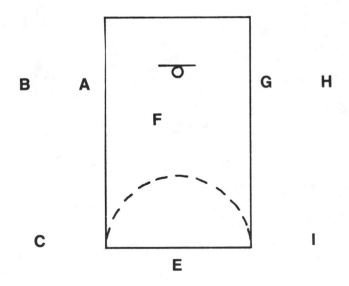

*Figure 66–1*

## Dave Lebo

*Carlisle High School*

In 1986–1987, during his twenty-first year of teaching, Dave Lebo became an overnight sensation when he directed Carlisle High School to its third straight Pennsylvania 4–A state title. Then, in 1988, the good news got better: Carlisle won an unprecedented fourth straight Pennsylvania title. Dave Lebo is as sound a fundamentalist as there is in the game. It's no accident that his son Jeff, a mainstay in the North Carolina backcourt, and Billy Owens, perhaps the best all-around high school player of the '80s, are two of the best shooters in America at their respective positions.

*Five-Star's version of "The Three Amigos": Dave Lebo (left), Billy Owens (right), and "The Legend," Frank Marino.*

Coach Dave Lebo
Carlisle High School
Carlisle, Pennsylvania

# 67. Spot Shooting Drill

Coach Lebo, a fundamental taskmaster, has stressed the "Spot Shooting Drill" and all his players have incorporated it into their practice routines. The quicker a player can shoot, the better chance he has of getting off the shot against pressurized defenses. Catching the ball off a spin out, squaring up, and releasing the jumper rapidly are the keys to success here. This is an excellent drill for a player to practice when he has no partner.

**Preparation:** Player stands in the perimeter region as shown in Figure 67–1.

1. Player holds the ball in both hands and faces the basket.

2. Player flips the ball, underhanded with some backspin, to one step right or left of where he is standing.

3. Player picks up the ball, stands in a ready position, shoots, and gets his own rebound.

4. Player takes the ball anywhere in the dotted line area and repeats steps 1–3.

**Points of Emphasis:**

- This is a continuous shooting drill designed to help players concentrate on the key elements of shooting. A minimum of ten minutes should be spent on the drill.

- The drill must be performed at game speed.

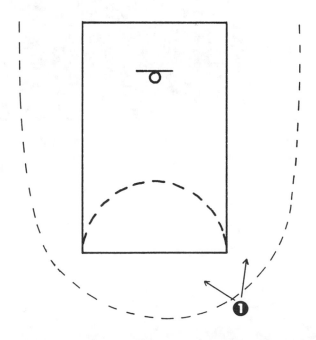

*Figure 67–1*

Coach Steve Lappas
Villanova University
Villanova, Pennsylvania

# 68. The DeBusschere Drill

Many players have difficulty recovering a loose ball at top speed and putting it back into play without committing a violation (walking, palming, double dribbling). In this drill, named for the former Knick Hall of Famer who obviously used it as one of his modes for shooting straight and quick and running all night, Coach Lappas creates two game situations: 1) recovering a loose ball and converting it into a layup, and 2) recovering a loose ball, squaring up immediately, and shooting. Use your imagination when creating the offensive move dictated in step 5.

**Preparation:** Player #1 stands out of bounds and player #2 stands at half court. Player #1 has the ball.

1. Player #1 passes the ball to player #2.

2. Player #1 sprints up court as player #2 rolls the ball up court.

3. Player #1 must catch the ball before it goes out of bounds. He then gathers himself and shoots the ball.

4. Player #1 gets his own rebound and both player #1 and player #2 cross to the other side of the court.

5. Steps 1-4 are repeated on the opposite side of the court with one change: when player #1 catches the ball after the roll he must make an offensive move and take one dribble before shooting.

6. Players reverse roles and repeat the drill.

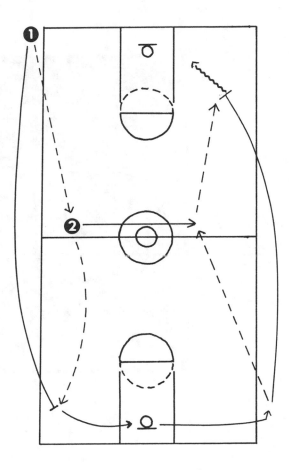

*Figure 68-1*

# Reneé Ackerman
*Champion High School*

Reneé Ackerman is considered the dean of Women's Five-Star. She was one of the first coaches hired and has helped Women's Five-Star become one of the top women's camps in the country. For fourteen years Reneé has coached at Champion High School in Warren, Ohio, where her teams have a combined record of 252 and 49. Champion High School has competed in the state of Connecticut for fourteen years straight, making the Final Sixteen six times. With three-time Coach of the Year winner Reneé Ackerman on board, it's no wonder we consider our women's staff one of the finest around.

Coach Reneé Ackerman
Champion High School
Warren, Ohio

# 69. Power Up Shot Drill

In today's women's basketball, most players are fundamentally sound at shooting the ball. However, many players are weak when it comes to shooting and scoring inside. The two following drills are part of a series designed to remedy this weakness. Remember, the team that has the ability to score inside is the team that wins the majority of its games.

**Preparation:** The coach has the ball and stands on the right side of the court (Figure 69-1). Player #1 is the defensive player and stands in the lane. Player #2 stands outside the lane on the right side of the court so that player #1 is directly behind her. Players #3, #4, and #5 line up behind the baseline.

1. Player #2 raises her baseline hand and the coach passes her the ball.

2. Player #2 executes a drop step by hooking her defensive leg.

3. Player #2 then dribbles, leaning into the basket, and makes a power layup with an optional head fake.

4. Players then repeat the drill by rotating positions clockwise: Player #1 goes to the end of the line behind player #5, player #2 moves to where player #1 was and acts as the defensive player, and player #3 takes player #2's position.

5. Players continue to rotate positions and repeat the drill until each player has played each position three times.

**Points of Emphasis:**

– Player #2 should get used to the feel of contact with player #1.

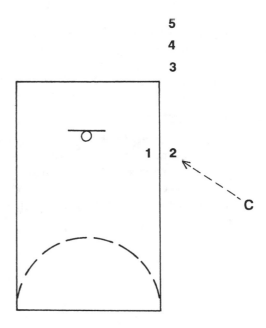

*Figure 69–1*

**Coach Reneé Ackerman**
**Champion High School**
**Warren, Ohio**

# 70. Pivot Shot Drill

**Preparation:** The coach has the ball and stands on the right side of the court (Figure 70–1). Player #2 stands to the right of the lane. Player #1 is the defensive player and stands between player #2 and the baseline. Players #3, #4, and #5 stand behind the baseline.

1. Player #2 raises her ball-side (right) hand. She pivots on her outside (right) foot clockwise, away from player #1.

2. Player #2 then squares up and shoots a jump shot.

3. If player #1 moves in front of player #2, player #2 steps to her left (non-pivot) foot, sealing off player #1. Player #2 then takes one dribble and makes a power layup to the basket.

4. Players then repeat the drill by rotating positoins clockwise: Player #1 goes to the end of the line behind player #5, player #2 moves to where player #1 was and acts as the defensive player, and player #3 takes player #2's position.

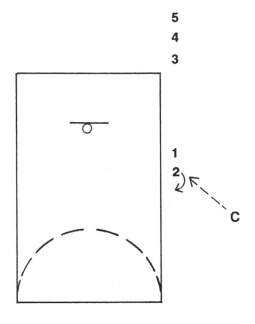

*Figure 70–1*

# Mitch Buonaguro
*Fairfield University*

One of the many problems with the three-point shot from the collegiate and high school twenty-one foot distance is that it masks the "legitimate" comebacks. Twenty-point turnarounds are as commonplace as an Iran-Contra indictment. Fairfield came from seventeen back with twelve minutes left in the Metro-Atlantic championship game to beat Iona in overtime. It was a comeback that could have occurred in 1907 or 1987 because it was practically void of the "three." But it was treated as just another night at the office by the media, and that's a shame for the game!

Mitch Buonaguro was named Co-Rookie Coach of the Year in 1985–1986 when he staged his first prestidigitation, miraculously moving the Stags from last to first in the MAAC and hanging tough with Illinois for thirty minutes. Mitch went from Five-Star camper to All-City at Bishop Loughlin to Boston College lead guard to BC grad assistant to Villanova full-timer, a tape-measure move credited to Rollie Massimino's gift for judging talent. Top recruiter, shrewd bench coach, tireless drillmaster, relentless teacher, and prolific speaker—that's Mitch Buonaguro, the whole package!

*Mitch Buonaguro coaching a defensive slide drill.*

**Coach Mitch Buonaguro**
**Fairfield University**
**Fairfield, Connecticut**

# 71. Jump Shot off the Jab Step Series Drill

Mitch Buonaguro's "Jump Shot off the Jab Step" was one of his many Morning Mini Lectures at Five-Star. One of the most fundamental one-on-one moves is the jab step series. A good jab step is executed when the lead foot is quickly jabbed at the defender's lead foot. The jab should be in a "heel-to-toe" relationship of no more than six to eight inches. The heel should extend beyond the pivot foot's toe. It would be ideal to get a layup off this move, but this isn't always feasible. So Coach Buonaguro stresses the jump shot off the jab step in four related drills.

**Preparation:** Player #1 stands at the top of the key. Player #2 has the ball and stands under the basket to act as a rebounder.

1. Player #2 passes the ball to player #1. Player #1 makes a quick jab step of about six to eight inches and goes up immediately for a jump shot (Figure 71-1).

2. Player #2 rebounds the ball and passes it back to player #1 who has returned to the top of the key.

3. Player #1 makes a quick jab step and then takes one dribble to his right for a quick jump shot (Figure 71-2).

4. Player #2 rebounds the ball and passes it back to player #1 who has returned to the top of the key.

5. Player #1 makes a quick jab step, takes two dribbles to his right, and shoots a bank shot (Figure 71-3).

6. Player #2 rebounds the ball and passes it back to player #1 who has returned to the top of the key.

7. Player #1 receives the ball in the triple threat position. Player #2 runs out at player #1. Player #1 uses a jab step to drive by player #2 for a quick jump shot (Figure 71-4).

8. Player #1 and player #2 exchange positions and repeat steps 1-7.

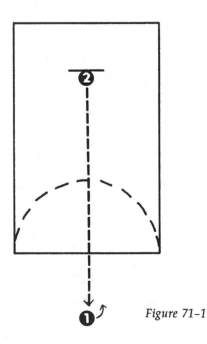

*Figure 71-1*

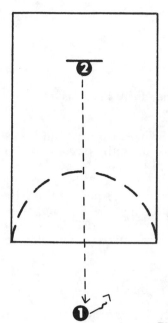

*Figure 71–2*

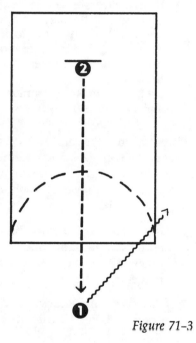

*Figure 71–3*

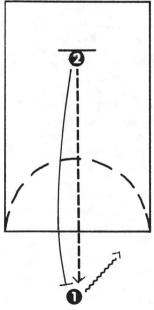

*Figure 71–4*

**Coach Hubie Brown**
**CBS-TV**

# 72. Fifty-Five-Second Drill

Bill Aberer describes his feelings about Hubie's classic "Fifty-Five-Second Drill" as follows:

> If ever one coach utilized time the best, it's Hubie Brown.  In this drill Coach Brown stresses several skills in one sequence.  To begin with, passing is emphasized.  The players practice three basic passes over a three-day period.  They are also learning how to feed the ball properly to the shooter, and the shooter is developing the technique of catching the ball off movement and squaring up to the hoop.  Finally, players are working under a fatigue factor—you are going to get tired if you do this drill properly.  What is remarkable about this drill is that you start out working primarily on your shooting, yet you are building several other skills at the same time.

**Preparation:**  Player #1 stands under the basket, player #2 stands at the foul line, and player #3 stands in the right wing.  Player #1 and player #2 each start in possession of a ball.

1.  In Formation 1 (Figure 72–1), player #1 rebounds all shots and pitches out to player #2.  Player #2 feeds the shooter, player #3.

2.  Player #3 must always V cut to get open.  Player #3 tries to get as many shots as possible in fifty-five seconds.

3.  Player #1 and player #2 exchange positions and repeat steps 1–7. After fifty-five seconds, players assume Formation 2 (Figure 72–2).  Players remain in the same positions on the court, but player #1 rebounds all shots and pitches out to player #3 who feeds the shooter, player #2.

4.  After another fifty-five seconds, players assume Formation 3 (Figure 72–3).  Player #1 rebounds all shots and pitches out to player #2 at the foul line.  Player #3 is the shooter and stands in the left wing.

**Points of Emphasis:**

– The object of the drill is to get as many shots in fifty-five seconds as possible, so the shooter cannot wait to see if the shot goes in but must immediately start his V cut after he releases his shot.

– The shooter should get behind the pass.

– The pass must be thrown to the inside shoulder (closest to the basket) to help the shooter get behind the pass.

– The catch should be made with the thumbs in a T position.

– Players should vary the passes they use, that is, they could use the chest pass on the first day, the bounce pass on the second day, and the overhead flick pass on the third day.

– Players should increase their range as they become proficient until they reach the twenty-one-foot line.

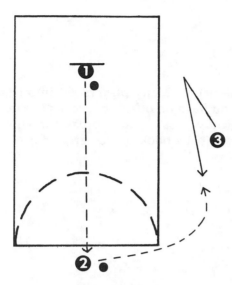

Figure 72–1

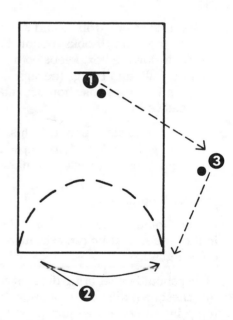

Figure 72–2

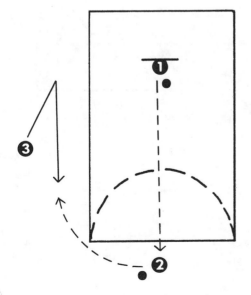

Figure 72—3

Coach Hubie Brown
CBS-TV

# 73. Baby Hook Drill

The toughest area to score in is the paint. Many players get into trouble because they break the lane, leave their feet, and have no offensive moves in the paint. Some players throw a "high degree of difficulty pass"; others break the lane and end up shooting a fade away shot. We teach the baby hook, which gives our players a strong offensive tool in the lane.

**Preparation:** Player stands at the broken circle.

1. Player takes one dribble and two steps to the right and hooks a shot. Player stays inside the box, keeps both hands on the ball, and brings the shot off his hip as he drops his shoulder into his defensive man.

2. Player repeats step 1, this time dribbling and taking two steps to the left and hooking the shot from the left.

**Points of Emphasis:**

– Player should always stay inside the box in the lane so that he can execute a hook off the glass.

– Player should never bring the shot across his chest, as this encourages a broad jump instead of a high jump.

– Player is encouraged to shoot off the hip and drop his shoulders because: 1) this gives him good vision to the box on the glass, 2) this enables him to put good back spin on the ball, and 3) upon release, his body will turn and give him good rebounding positioning.

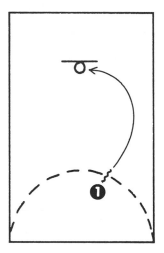

*Figure 73–1*

Figure 73-2

*Hubie Brown, one of the top color analysts on TV, still active in Five-Star affairs. Here he delivers his "Gettysburg Address" to June '87 campers.*

[Top] "Good Mourning, America":
The so-called "dead period" comes alive
in Honesdale's late August session.
John Wooden award-winner Alonzo
Mourning (center) leads a galaxy of
stars.

[Left] Billy Owens, the "Baryshnikov
of Basketball," is considered by many
the high school player of the decade.

# John Calipari
*University of Pittsburgh*

Success wrapped its arms around John Calipari and won't let go. "The harder I work, the luckier I get" is his theme song. He chirped his way onto Larry Brown's staff at Kansas and the Jayhawks soared. The Pittsburgh native returned home with Roy Chipman and remained when Paul Evans took over the reins in 1986–1987. Like the Pied Piper at his best, Calipari whistled a happy tune to four of the nation's finest prep stars and they followed. One of them, Brian Shorter of Philadelphia, played string music for 2,523 career points, bursting Wilt Chamberlain's 2,252 balloons though Shorter's last 654 were meshed at Oak Hill Academy in Virginia. Bobby Martin's (Atlantic City High School) last-second switch from Villanova to Pitt caused the biggest uproar since Oliver North said, "Sold!" And 6'0'' Sean Miller might be the quarterback the Panthers need to stay at or near the top of the national heap for years to come. If he isn't, 6'3'' Jason Matthews, a defensive shark out of Santa Monica, California, will surprise the critics who say he can't shoot.

There is no way that John Calipari can be typed as just a recruiter. His innovative stations and freewheeling coaching style, nurtured during his playing days at UNC-Wilmington and Clarion State, are part of Five-Star lore, especially his work with the rising sophomore Development Leaguers during the usually loaded Pitt-1 session. We're sure he has told them about his "Thirty-Minute Shooting Workout." Now it's time to practice.

**Coach John Calipari**
**University of Pittsburgh**
**Pittsburgh, Pennsylvania**

The following five quick drills comprise Coach Calipari's "Thirty-Minute Shooting Workout."

# 74. Straight Shots Drill

**Preparation:**  Player #1 serves as the rebounder and stands underneath the basket.  Player #2 stands at the top of the key. Player #1 has the ball.

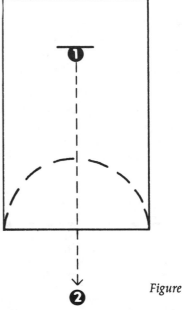

1.  Player #1 throws a chest pass to player #2.

2.  Player #2 gets his hands and body ready to shoot as soon as the pass is made.

3.  Player #2 catches the ball and takes a shot.

4.  Players continue in this manner until player #2 has taken a total of fifty shots in five sets of ten.

**Points of Emphasis:**

– Player #2 should not dip as he shoots the ball.

*Figure 74–1*

*Woody Williams, of Lake Clifton High School, in his famous pass blocking drill at Five-Star.*

*Will Klein, Five-Star's co-director, at his one and only lecture at the inaugural session of Five-Star in 1966 at Niverville, New York. Klein is the principal of Evander Childs High School in Bronx, New York.*

Coach John Calipari
University of Pittsburgh
Pittsburgh, Pennsylvania

# 75. Wing to Wing Drill

**Preparation:**  Player #1 has the ball and stands underneath the basket.  Player #2 stands at the left elbow.

1. Player #2 moves from the left elbow to the right elbow.

2. Player #1 throws the ball to player #2 as soon as player #2 reaches the right elbow.

3. Player #2 squares up to the basket, plants his inside foot, and takes a shot.

4. Steps 1–3 are repeated, as player #2 moves from elbow to elbow, until he has taken a total of fifty shots in five sets of ten.

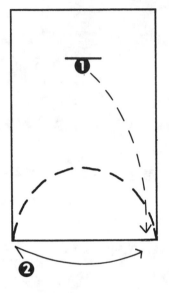

*Figure 75–1*

Coach John Calipari
University of Pittsburgh
Pittsburgh, Pennsylvania

# 76. Ball Fake Drill

**Preparation:** Player #1 has the ball and stands underneath the basket. Player #2 stands at the left elbow.

1. Player #2 moves to the right elbow, catches a pass from player #1, and fakes a shot.

2. Player #2 crosses over into the lane and takes one dribble.

3. Player #2 takes a shot from within the lane.

4. Steps 1–3 are repeated, as player #2 moves from elbow to elbow, until he has taken a total of fifty shots in five sets of ten.

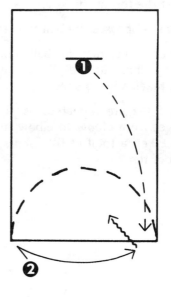

*Figure 76–1*

Coach John Calipari
University of Pittsburgh
Pittsburgh, Pennsylvania

# 77. One-Two Dribbles Drill

**Preparation:**  Player #1 has the ball and stands underneath the basket.  Player #2 stands at the top of the key.

1. Player #1 passes the ball to player #2.

2. Player #2 catches the ball, takes one hard dribble to the elbow, pulls up, and takes a jump shot.

3. Steps 1–2 are repeated, as player #2 moves from elbow to elbow, until he has taken a total of fifty shots in five sets of ten.

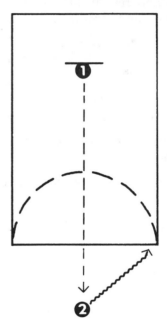

*Figure 77–1*

Coach John Calipari
University of Pittsburgh
Pittsburgh, Pennsylvania

# 78. Distract the Shooter Drill

**Preparation:**  Player #1 has the ball. Player #1 stands underneath the basket and serves as rebounder. Player #2 stands at the top of the key.

1. Player #1 passes the ball to player #2.

2. Player #2 squares up as player #1 runs at player #2 and tries to distract him by holding his hand up and yelling.

3. Steps 1–2 are repeated until player #2 has taken a total of fifty shots in five sets of ten.

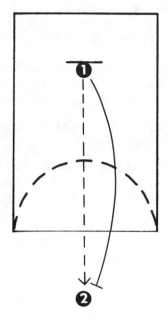

*Figure 78–1*

Coach Rick Pitino
New York Knicks
New York, New York

# 79. Two-Man Shooting Drill

In this drill Coach Pitino teaches his players to catch, square up, and shoot under pressure. Shooting under pressure, or with a hand in your face, is the ultimate way to practice your shooting techniques. The element of fatigue is a factor in this drill—as the drill progresses, you will become tired and that's when you truly begin to learn and gain inner strength.

**Preparation:** Player #1 stands under the basket and player #2 stands in the corner (position A in Figure 79–1).

1. Player #1 throws a chest pass to player #2 (Figure 79–1).

2. Player #2 stands in an athletic position (Figure 79–2). He catches the ball ready to shoot (Figure 79–3).

3. Player #1 tries to block player #2's shot. He does not run by player #2 but simply runs out with a hand up (Figure 79–4).

4. Player #2 shoots and rebounds his own shot as player #1 moves to the corner (position A) and prepares himself to be ready to shoot (Figure 79–5).

5. Player #2 throws a chest pass to player #1 and the players switch places and repeat the drill.

6. Players then perform steps 1–5 from positions B through I in Figure 79–1.

**Points of Emphasis:**

– In step 3 player #1 runs out with a hand up instead of running by player #2 so that he can avoid the bad habit of going for ball fakes and getting beaten.

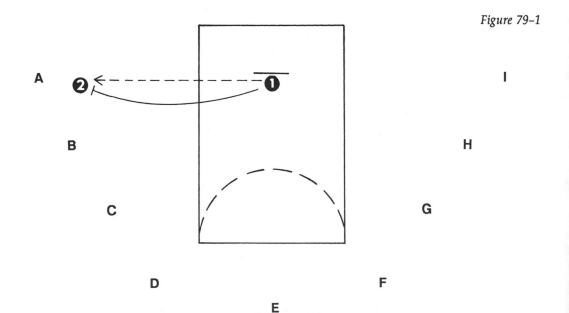

*Figure 79–1*

*Figure 79–2*

*Figure 79–3*

*Figure 79–4*

*Figure 79–5*

*"Two Man Shooting Drill" in action at Five-Star: Oklahoma's Tim McAlister shoots from the corner as Ohio's Dave Jamerson makes a mock attempt to block the shot. To the right of Coach Rick Pitino is Ohio State's Dennis Hopson, the third overall pick in the 1987 NBA draft, who went to the New Jersey Nets.*

Coach Rick Pitino
New York Knicks
New York, New York

# 80. Two-Man Shooting Drill With Ball Fake

Here Coach Pitino expands on his "Two-Man Shooting Drill." When you are comfortable with the original drill, it is time to start developing a few more skills. In this drill Coach Pitino allows you to use ball fakes to explode past your defender, thereby mirroring a typical game situation. Coach Pitino insists that players perform all his drills at game speed after mastering them at a slower, learning pace. Don't be frightened by the terminology "ball-quick." This is one of Pitino's favorite phrases and being ball-quick will come with practice and experience. You can be ball-quick without being fast or strong—and you will score!

**Preparation:** Player #1 stands under the basket and player #2 stands in the corner (position A in Figure 80–1). Player #1 has the ball.

1. Player #1 throws a chest pass to player #2 (Figure 80–1).

2. Player #2 catches the ball ready to shoot in an athletic position as player #1 runs at him.

3. Player #2 has two options: 1) He can ball fake and explode by the defender for a jump shot, using at most two dribbles, or 2) He can ball fake, swing the ball across his body, and cross over in front of the defender for a jump shot.

4. Player #2 rebounds his own shot, and player #1 moves to the corner (position A).

5. Player #2 throws a chest pass to player #1, and the players switch places and repeat the drill.

6. Players then perform steps 1–5 from positions B through I in Figure 80–1.

**Points of Emphasis for the Ball Fake**

– The player should pull the ball close to his body.

– The player should keep his eyes fixed on the rim of the basket.

– The player should ball fake with an act: he stays down, and the ball comes up; if the player is crossing over, he ball fakes and then swings the ball around his body. The player must be ball-quick.

– The player should bounce the ball below his waist, stay low, and step by the defender. His hip should almost touch the defender's hip. He should go directly toward the basket rather than moving laterally.

– The defender must slide with the shooter and challenge the shot.

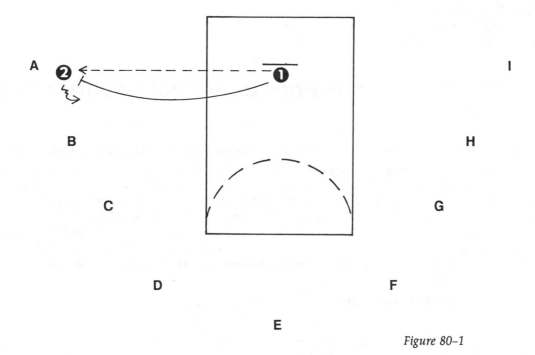

*Figure 80-1*

*Rick Pitino teaching Kenny Hutchinson (University of Arkansas) one-on-one moves.*

Coach Rick Pitino
New York Knicks
New York, New York

# 81. Plus Four Minus Four Beat Your Favorite Pro Drill

The six "Plus Four Minus Four" drills are designed to provide players with a competitive, up-tempo, and pressure-packed shooting session. Coach Pitino gives you a great opportunity to work on your "ball-quickness" as well as your shots from various spots on the floor. Once again the fatigue factor is present. Players who can shoot—and make the shot—when they are tired and under pressure are good shooters. If you "beat your favorite pro" legitimately, you are a whale of a shooter! For instance, Coach Pitino himself, who has become a terrific shooter in his "old age," has rarely beaten Larry Bird in his Five-Star Camp attempts. Maybe next time he'll try Dale Ellis.

**Preparation:** Player stands under the basket.

1. Player tosses the ball with backspin toward the right corner within his shooting range (Figure 81-1).

2. Player sprints in front of the ball so that when it bounces he is facing the basket. He must be sure to turn as if he is receiving a pass from the wing or the top of the key area.

3. Player catches the ball off the first bounce and pulls the ball back into his shooting pocket (that is, directly above his shooting-side hip) as quickly as possible.

4. Player shoots the ball. He scores one point if he makes the basket, and he loses two points if he misses the basket.

5. Player sprints and rebounds his shot.

6. Player repeats steps 1-5 from the left corner (Figure 81-2).

7. Player continues moving from corner to corner until he reaches a score of plus four or minus four.

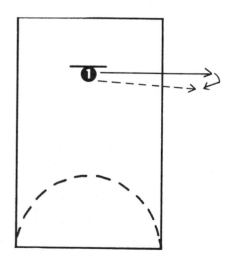

*Figure 81-1*

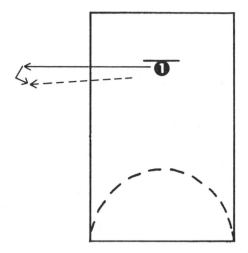

*Figure 81–2*

*Rick Pitino will lead the New York Knicks to the Promised Land.*

**Coach Rick Pitino**
**New York Knicks**
**New York, New York**

# 82. Plus Four Minus Four Bank Shot Drill

**Preparation:** Player stands under the basket.

1. Player tosses the ball with backspin to the right of the lane (Figure 82–1).

2. Player sprints in front of the ball so that when it bounces he is facing the basket.

3. Player catches the ball off the first bounce and pulls the ball back into his shooting pocket (i.e., directly above his shooting-side hip) as quickly as possible.

4. Player shoots a bank shot. He scores one point if he makes the basket and loses two points if he misses the basket.

5. Player sprints and rebounds his shot.

6. Player repeats steps 1–5 from the left side of the court.

7. Player continues moving from the left to the right side of the court until he reaches a score of plus four or minus four.

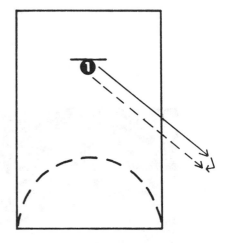

*Figure 82–1*

**Points of Emphasis:**

– When he shoots the bank shot, player must be sure to stay above the box to insure the proper angle.

Coach Rick Pitino
New York Knicks
New York, New York

# 83. Plus Four Minus Four Curl the Elbow Drill

**Preparation:** Player stands under the basket.

1. Player tosses the ball with backspin toward the right elbow.

2. Player curls outside the lane, sprinting in front of the ball, and catches the ball on one bounce at the elbow. He faces the basket and pulls the ball back into his shooting pocket (i.e., directly above his shooting-side hip) as quickly as possible.

3. Player shoots the ball. He scores one point if he makes the basket and loses two points if he misses the basket.

4. Player sprints and rebounds his shot.

5. Player repeats steps 1–4 from the left elbow.

6. Player continues moving from the left to the right elbow and back until he reaches a score of plus four or minus four.

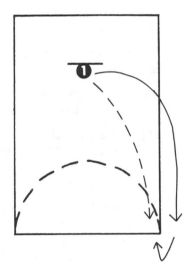

*Figure 83–1*

*The theory is, if you can make 'em from here, you can make 'em from anywhere.*

Coach Rick Pitino
New York Knicks
New York, New York

# 84. Plus Four Minus Four Side of the Key Drill

**Preparation:** Player stands under the basket.

1. Player dribbles out to the left top of the key extended area.

2. Player jump stops and pivots so that he faces the key.

3. Player throws a pass with backspin toward the left side of the key.

4. Player sprints in front of the ball so that when it bounces he is facing the basket. He must not cross the imaginary line that dissects the court.

5. Player catches the ball off the first bounce and pulls the ball back into his shooting pocket (i.e., directly above his shooting-side hip) as quickly as possible.

6. Player shoots the ball. He scores one point if he makes the basket and loses two points if he misses the basket.

7. Player sprints and rebounds his shot.

8. Player repeats steps 1–7 from the right side of the court.

9. Player continues moving from the left to the right side of the court and back until he reaches a score of plus four or minus four.

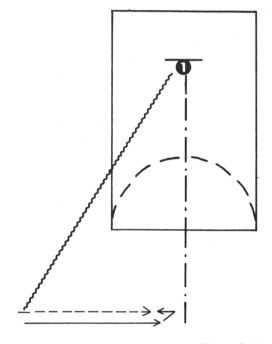

*Figure 84–1*

Coach Rick Pitino
New York Knicks
New York, New York

# 85. Plus Four Minus Four Cross the Key Drill

**Preparation:** Player stands under the basket.

1. Player dribbles out to the left top of key extended area.

2. Player jump stops and pivots so that he faces the key.

3. Player throws a pass with backspin toward the left side of the key.

4. Player sprints in front of the ball so that when it bounces he is facing the basket. He should sprint far enough so that he crosses the imaginary line that dissects the court.

5. Player catches the ball off the first bounce and pulls the ball back into his shooting pocket (that is, directly above his shooting-side hip) as quickly as possible.

6. Player shoots the ball. He scores one point if he makes the basket and loses two points if he misses the basket.

7. Player sprints and rebounds his shot.

8. Player repeats steps 1–7 from the right side of the court.

9. Player continues moving from the left to the right side of the court and back until he reaches a score of plus four or minus four.

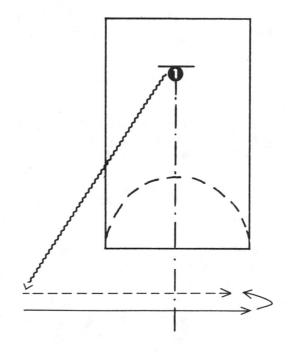

*Figure 85–1*

# Jamie Ciampaglio

*University of Rhode Island*

John Wooden once told us that in his opinion most basketball games are won off the boards. We're not about to debate the "Wizard of Westwood," who won ten national championships and is the only person in history to have entered the "Hall of Fame" as both a player and a coach! But here's an observation from the editor of *Five-Star Basketball Drills*: more close games are *lost* on the foul line than anywhere else. The fifteen-foot charity stripe is a devil's playground even for talented shooters and sheer hell for the undisciplined. Jimmy Valvano won a national title by daring the Houston Cougars to make a free throw. If Wilt Chamberlain, who shot around fifty percent from the line for most of his career, had been an adept free-thrower, they would have had to change the rules to accommodate his talent. Like one point for a dunk? Hey, that's not a bad idea anyway.

Jamie Ciampaglio has written the most comprehensive thesis on free throw shooting you'll ever read. So read it! It can't do anything but help you. Prior to taking assistant coaching jobs with Rick Pitino at Boston U and now with Tom Peters at Rhodie, Jamie was named metropolitan New York's Collegiate Player of the Year after his senior year at Wagner College under P. J. Carlesimo. "The Man with the Golden Arm" could—and still can—shoot. At one time he spent twenty-five consecutive sessions at Five-Star during his undergraduate days, so he's heard and learned from the best. The most important thing to remember is that you can improve your foul shooting if you work at it! Ciampaglio particularly works at it in early August with the more than two hundred girls who attend his Five-Star Women's Camp at Coraopolis, Pennsylvania.

*Jamie Ciampaglio (center) as a Five-Star camper.*

Coach Jamie Ciampaglio
University of Rhode Island
Kingston, Rhode Island

# 86. Foul Shooting Drill

**Preparation:** Player #1 stands at the foul line directly in front of the basket. Player #2 stands at his side.

1. Player #1 places his lead foot on the foul line, bends his knees, and assumes a comfortable stance.

2. Player #1 shoots from the foul line.

3. After taking the shot, player #1 steps back and then approaches the line again.

4. Player #1 shoots from the foul line.

5. Player #1 repeats steps 1–4 until he has made two foul shots. The two players then switch positions, and player #2 performs steps 1–4.

6. The two players continue in this fashion, switching positions each time a player makes two foul shots. The drill ends when each player has made two foul shots fifteen times.

**Points of Emphasis:**

– Players must not talk while performing this drill.

– The shooter should place the middle finger of his shooting hand on the ball. He should spread his fingers wide so the pads of his fingers are the only part of his hand touching the ball.

– The shooter's guide hand should be placed on the side of the ball and the thumb of his guide hand should form a T with the thumb of his shooting hand.

– The shooter should tuck in his elbow so that it is directly under the ball.

– Players should be discouraged from bouncing the ball before shooting it.

– The shooter should take a deep breath before beginning his shooting routine.

– The shooter should fix his eyes on the rim and imagine the ball going in.

– As he shoots, the player should place his lead foot on the foul line directly in front of the rim.

– The shooting motion should be as follows: 1) player dips and bends his knees; 2) player straightens up, brings the ball over his head with his elbow pointing toward the hoop; and 3) player releases the ball, locking his elbows, snapping his wrist downward, and reaches toward the basket.

– Upon release of the ball, the player's middle finger should be pointing toward the floor.

– As player approaches the line, he should wipe off his hands on the backs of his socks.

– The routine is very important. The player should be in the habit of shooting his free throws the same way every time.

# PART SIX:

# REBOUNDING DRILLS

# George Raveling
*University of Southern California*

If ten people who know him even a little were given a word association test on George Raveling, five would say "rebounding" and five would say "recruiting." That's the price he must pay for writing the definitive work on rebounding, *War on the Boards*, and for revolutionizing the recruiting system for collegiate basketball players in this country. In 1960 George received his doctorate in retrieving from Villanova, where he was captain and All-American and played in the East-West College All-Star game. He was also voted Senior Student of the Year and received a degree in economics.

George's love affair with legal-sized yellow paper (he and Richard Nixon kept those people in business for years) began in 1963 under Jack Kraft at Nova and continued with Lefty Dreisell at Maryland in 1970—when he became the first black coach in the ACC. Some of the names that appeared on those legendary sheets of yellow paper that helped build the Wildcats and Terps into national powers were Howard Porter, Tom McMillen, Len Elmore, John Lucas, and Jap Trimble.

Then in 1972 George was appointed head coach at Washington State of the Pac-10 and in short order put Pullman on the basketball map. "Ravs" came up big in 1983 and 1984 as boss of the Iowa Hawkeyes and as assistant under Bob Knight on the USA's gold medal Olympic team, respectively. Then it was back to the yellow paper: Roy Marble, Al Lorenzen, B. J. Armstrong, Ed Horton, Kevin Gamble, and Jeff Moe. On the brink of Iowa's surge into the Top Ten at the end of the 1986 season, Raveling departed for the warmth of Southern California, a Pac-10 encore. As long as he doesn't run out of legal paper, the Trojans are a live horse.

*George Raveling shows how to make friends with a basketball.*

Coach George Raveling
University of Southern California
Los Angeles, California

# 87. Superman Drill

Raveling's fifteen years with Five-Star—and he's now a permanent member of our lecture force—are among the most memorable in camp history. His closing day oratory, a cross between the Gettysburg Address and the Sermon on the Mount, is a motivational classic. So is his "Superman Drill," which he introduced at Five-Star in 1973. It's still a highlight of our rebounding stations and of others across the country. This is a physically demanding routine that can't help but improve your strength, stamina, and timing. It also will help you snare the big rebound in the big game.

**Preparation:** Player stands on the right lane midpoint.

1. Player tosses the ball high off the backboard slightly to the left of the basket.

2. Player takes one step into the lane and catches the ball outside the lane on the left side as he faces the basket. He must make a power jump in order to propel himself to the other side of the lane.

**Points of Emphasis:**

– The drill should be repeated twenty-five times.

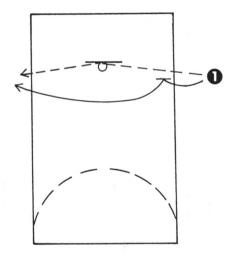

*Figure 87–1*

Coach George Raveling
University of Southern California
Los Angeles, California

# 88. Two-Man Volleyball Drill

Coach Raveling, whose second book, *A Rebounder's Workshop,* is now in its second printing, concentrates on a few of the essentials needed to be a good rebounder. Coach Raveling emphasizes the bounce jump rather than taking a step and then leaping, an important point which is often overlooked. And once again, timing is stressed more than leaping ability.

**Preparation:** Player #1 has the ball and stands on the right box. Player #2 stands on the left box.

1. Player #1 tosses the ball off the opposite (left) corner of the backboard.

2. Player #2 jumps up, rebounds the ball and, while still in the air, throws it back to the opposite (right) side of the backboard.

3. Player #1 jumps up, rebounds the ball and, while still in the air, throws it back to the opposite (left) side of the backboard.

4. The two players continue in this manner for sixty seconds.

**Points of Emphasis:**

– Players must remember to rebound off their toes.

– Players should keep their arms above their shoulders and their heads up as they rebound.

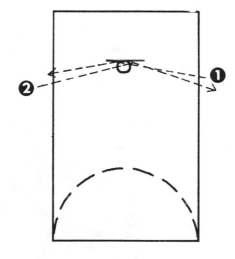

*Figure 88-1*

# Bill Aberer

*La Salle Academy*

The scene is the Roy Rubin Basketball School in Niverville, New York, and Bill Aberer sits mesmerized by the likes of Hubie Brown, Marv Kessler, Chuck Daly, Danny Buckley (La Salle Academy and King's Point), and Mike Cingiser (Brown). The time is 1965 and "Coach" was a camper in our first NIT and a student at La Salle. Very little has changed in twenty-three years. Aberer is still in the NIT and still at La Salle. The difference is that he's now the commissioner of the league in June and August and the head coach of the Cardinals. The latter was a long time coming, but Bill persevered—just the way he teaches!

We clearly remember an Aberer-coached NBA championship five, Staff Day lectures *par excellence*, and if his rising sophomore-junior league isn't the best-organized each week he runs it, he flips. His artwork is now legendary: those neat "Standings of the Clubs" charts that adorn the Five-Star walls each session and the technically correct preliminary diagrams he prepared for this book are just two examples.

Coach Bill Aberer
La Salle Academy
New York, New York

# 89. Offensive Rebounding Versus Pressure Drill

How many times have you heard someone say, "I missed the shot because he pushed me," or "He held me and the ref didn't see it"?  Under the boards things get rough, and only the tough survive.  Bearing this in mind, Coach Aberer has developed a drill to encompass a situation in which a player must rebound and score with someone pressuring him from behind.  The defender tries to stop him any way he can!

**Preparation:**  Player #1 has the ball and stands on the foul line to the right of the basket.  Player #2 stands directly behind player #1.

1.  Player #1 throws the ball underhanded off the right side of the backboard.

2.  Player #1 explodes to the ball and rebounds with two hands above his head.  He then comes down, keeping the ball at shoulder level or above.

3.  Player #2 stays directly behind player #1 during the rebounding sequence.

4.  Player #1 now pump fakes (violent head and shoulders fake) and powers up for a layup.

5.  Player #2 must put pressure on player #1 while player #1 attempts to score.  Player #2 may do this by bumping or pushing player #1.

6.  Each player attempts ten shots from both the right and left sides of the court.

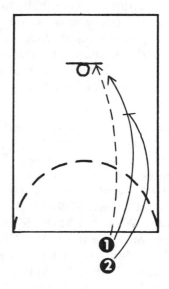

*Figure 89–1*

# Bob Wade
*University of Maryland*

There's a lot to be proud of in the twenty-three years of Five-Star, but nothing matches the one hundred men (an average of more than four per year) who began on our staff as high school coaches or college players and moved ahead to college and/or pro coaching positions. Eleven have gone on to coach in the NBA, and we're still counting! The one hundredth such coach, a milestone in Five-Star history, was Bob "Sugar" Wade, who was named head coach of the Maryland Terps in the fall of 1986.

The Wade success story—and it's really only beginning—is truly an amazing saga. The man was born and bred to play and coach football. His hoops are self-taught, and what a great teacher he must be. His football teams were good, and his basketball teams were great! Wade was drafted out of Morgan State by the Baltimore Colts in 1967 and spent four years in the NFL as a defensive back with the Redskins, Steelers, and Broncos. His career was cut short by a wrist injury, and basketball was the winner—Baltimore basketball, to be precise. In 1975 he found Dunbar High School, and hoop history was about to be made. Dunbar in Washington, D. C. was developing supers, and Wade wanted a piece of the action. Not that Dunbar-Baltimore hadn't had its share of great ones—Skip Wise and Larry Gibson weren't exactly chopped liver. Yet despite roof-ratings on these players from HSBI Report, Baltimore remained in the Rodney Dangerfield mold—it got no respect. Then came Wade and Five-Star.

Sugar's first one was Ernest Graham. In rapid succession came David Wingate, Reggie Williams, Tyrone (Mugsy) Bogues, Reggie Lewis, the Dozier twins, and others—the names could fill this page. So could the titles. The "Reign of Terror" included an undefeated 1981–1982 campaign, a #2 *USA-Today* ranking, and national championships in 1982-1983 and 1984–1985 (USA's/Dave Krider's #1 club both years). Along with close friend Woody Williams (Lake Clifton High School), he built Five-Star's Pitt-3 into "Baltimore Week," a haven for some of the best players in America. Bob was also an organizational giant for the Nike Academic Camp in Princeton, New Jersey. His recruiting talents must have impressed Lefty Dreisell, the master he replaced: first-team *Basketball Times* All-American center 6'10'' Brian Williams and everyone's favorite Juco guard, Rudy Archer from Allegany C.C.

*Stars of "Baltimore Week": Bob "Sugar" Wade (left), the Dunbar High School coach, and close pal Woody Williams, of Lake Clifton High School. Wade became the one-hundredth Five-Star resident coach to move from high school to the collegiate or professional coaching ranks. He became head coach at the University of Maryland in November 1986, succeeding Lefty Dreisell.*

Coach Bob Wade
University of Maryland
Baltimore, Maryland

# 90. Power Up Drill

Coach Wade's "Power-Up Drill" deals with rebounding in traffic and powering up against pressure at its best. It separates the men from the boys in the constant war waged in the paint. Both aspects are featured, to say the least. The retriever gets to work against a defender who faces him. This forces the rebounder to work on some fundamental moves, such as head and shoulders fakes and pivotal moves, while the defender gets more than a workout.

**Preparation:** Player #1 has the ball and stands in the lane on the right side. Player #2 stands out of bounds on the right side.

1. Player #1 tosses the ball high off the backboard.

2. Player #2 steps on the floor as soon as the ball hits the board.

3. Player #1 rebounds the ball with two hands above his head.

4. Player #1 must try to score over player #2 by using ball fake or pivot moves. He may take a maximum of one dribble.

5. Play continues until player #1 scores or until player #2 stops him.

6. At this point the players exchange positions, and play continues until a player scores three baskets.

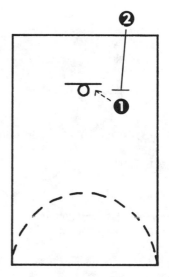

*Figure 90–1*

# Warren Isaac

*Di Varese Basketball Association*

We first saw Warren Isaac operate at the Jack Donahue Basketball Camp ("Friendship Farm") almost twenty-six years ago. He was a junior at Iona College and about to lead the nation's rebounders (12.2 average) in his senior year. He practiced what he preached, and no one has ever taught it better. If Isaac could have shot it, he would have been an NBA journeyman for years. Instead he made his mark in the Italian Pro League as a player and coach and is now coaching and helping direct affairs. The United States is missing a good one. We know because he was extraordinary at Five-Star for three years. He coached an NBA championship team and was the "Elmer Gantry of Rebounding" at Five-Star stations.

*Warren Isaac demonstrates how to hold a man off with one finger (the "one-finger box-out"). Camper Mark Cline, star forward at Wake Forest University, looks like he's ticklish.*

Coach Warren Isaac
Di Varese Basketball Association
(Italian Professional League)
Varese, Italy

# 91. Tip Rebounding Drill

Warren Isaac's "Tip Rebounding Drill" is designed to include all the basics needed to board and pitch. It also emphasizes a skill very rarely practiced or taught—a typical Isaac innovation. Many times you cannot grab a "clean" carom so it's necessary to "keep the ball alive" or tap it to yourself in a more open spot. Too many times a player will be called for "over the top" because he's never worked on the art of tapping the ball out of the lane or congested area. This drill is perfect for developing that concept and for adding to the savvy of a rebounder.

**Preparation:** Player #1 has the ball and stands at the right side of the foul line. Player #2 stands off to the right of player #1. It is assumed that player #1 cannot come down with a two-handed rebound.

1.  Player #1 throws the ball underhanded off the backboard (Figure 91–1).

2.  Player #1 tips the ball to a spot where he can retrieve it.

3.  Player #1 retrieves the tip rebound with two hands extended above his head and quickly turns to the outlet side.

4.  Player #1 throws an outlet pass (a two-handed over-the-head pass) to player #2 who receives the ball with his back facing the sideline (Figure 91–2).

5.  Player #1 sprints to the outlet area while player #2 dribbles to the foul line.

6.  Player #1 and player #2 exchange roles and repeat steps 1–5.

7.  Each player should rebound ten times, change sides of the floor, and repeat the drill.

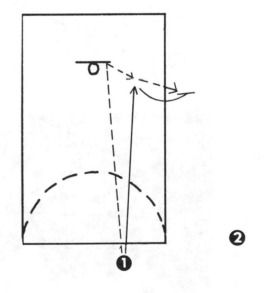

*Figure 91–1*

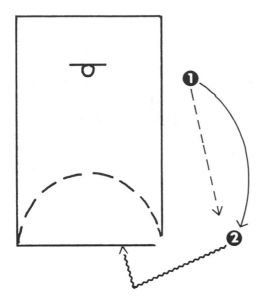

*Figure 91–2*

*Jim Boheim (left) and Bob Knight, 1986–1987 NCAA Tourney finalists, renew "old times" in a July 1987 reunion at a prospect-laden Pitt-1 session.*

## Dick Ponti

*Kempsville High School*

Dick Ponti joined the Five-Star family one year after J. R. Reid starred in the Development League.  He remains one of the easiest coaches on the staff to introduce. You merely say "Here's the man who taught J. R. how to play."  Dick gains instant credibility, especially with the big guys.  It reminds us of Jimmy Stewart in *The Man Who Shot Liberty Valance*—the guns are put away and the attention span doubles.  And why not?  Reid was the 1986–1987 ACC Rookie of the Year, Al McGuire's Freshman of the Year, and someday may even be a role model.  One of Ponti's other winners at Kempsville was Penn State's star running back D. J. Dozier, an all-district hoopster, who scored the winning TD against Miami in the Sugar Bowl to maintain Nittany's number one ranking.  Ponti has had problems finding another superstar.  Nobody's enrolled at his school with a first name composed of initials.

After transferring from Morrisville College, the 6'6" Ponti found a home in Virginia, and his forty-five points in a single game still stand as a school record.  After eight years at Kempsville he has compiled a 120–68 won-lost log and has five district championships notched on his belt.

*Overview of morning stations at Five-Star.*

Coach Dick Ponti
Kempsville High School
Virginia Beach, Virginia

# 92. Offensive Stick Back Drill

Here are some thoughts on Coach Ponti's effective "Offensive Stick Back Drill." Players have a habit of rebounding and hurrying their shot to avoid contact. We want contact, and the "violent pump fake," as Chuck Daly used to say, accomplishes two things: 1) the rebounder can now gather himself and take it up strong to the iron, and 2) he is developing the habit of bringing the leaper down to size. The chances of a three-point play are thereby increased.

**Preparation:** Player #1 has the ball and stands on the right box. Player #2 stands on the left box. Player #1 is the shooter, and player #2 is the offensive rebounder. Player #3 positions himself next to player #2 as a defensive player.

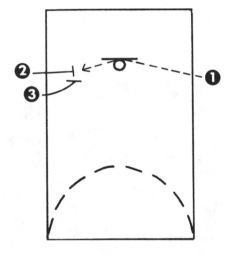

1. Player #1 deliberately misses a bank shot from the box so the ball can be rebounded on the other side of the basket.

2. Player #2 rebounds the ball, gives a violent pump fake, and attempts a shot. Player #2 must keep the ball above his head to avoid being stripped.

3. Player #3 allows player #2 to rebound. Then player #3 gives resistance to the shot.

4. After the shot attempt, the three players rotate positions and repeat the drill.

*Figure 92–1*

*J. R. Reid wins the tip during a Pitt-1 playoff championship game.*

# PART SEVEN:

# DEFENSE DRILLS

# Joe Petrocelli
*Bishop Alter High School*

Little did Joe Petrocelli realize that when he sent Jim Paxson to Honesdale in 1974, he was starting a revolution. Paxson must have liked what he saw, because the following summer twenty-five campers came from Ohio. A bunch of Michiganians were also present due to the influence of Tom LaGarde (North Carolina, Denver, and Seattle), who had come to Five-Star two years earlier. Our horizons were expanding and suddenly there were New York City kids on the waiting list. Hello, Wheeling, West Virginia.

"Petro's" influence on basketball extends a lot farther than Honesdale, Pennsylvania or Kettering, Ohio, home of famed Bishop Alter High School. In twenty-three years of head coaching, he has sent forty of his players to major colleges, won 408 games against 103 losses, won the Triple A state title in 1978, captured nine district and two regional tournaments, and seized so many holiday crowns that part of the school's trophy chest is now a closet.

Coach Joe Petrocelli
Bishop Alter High School
Kettering, Ohio

# 93. The Tube Defensive Slide Drill

Although most of the drills in this book were either introduced or taught by the coaches at Five-Star, Joe's "Tube Drill," because of logistics, was not. John Paxson, who is currently lighting it up for the Chicago Bulls and is a member of Five-Star's unofficial "Hall of Fame," demonstrates this drill at the Alter Basketball Camp, which "Petro" and he operate. It's an exercise you can do alone, and we thought it would make an imaginative opening to our defensive section. In order to play solid defense, you must be comfortable in your stance. If your legs aren't accustomed to the stress that this position will put on them, you will tire quickly. You'll be amazed at the way this drill will make your legs (especially your ankles) stronger and your footwork improve.

**Preparation:** Player obtains an old inner tube or piece of elastic two to four inches wide and about twenty-four inches long. If he uses elastic, he should tie the ends of the elastic together to form a circle. He then slips the tube around his calves just above the ankles. The tube should be tied so that when it is stretched fairly tightly the player's feet are twelve inches apart.

1. Player stands on the right side of the foul line and assumes a good defensive stance.

2. Player step slides, using the stretch of the tube, and moves across the lane until he reaches the left end of the foul line.

3. Player then returns to the right side of the lane using the step slide technique.

4. Player continues in this manner for ten minutes.

**Points of Emphasis:**

– The drill should be performed at a slow pace to enable the player to feel the pull of the tube on his legs.

– This drill promotes leg strength and improves foot movement.

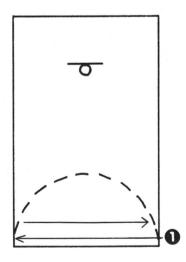

*Figure 93–1*

# Mike Krzyzewski
*Duke University*

Leo Durocher, arguably the greatest baseball manager who ever lived, once said, "Nice guys finish last." It's still a famous quote, and it's still wrong! Obviously, Leo never met Mike Krzyzewski. The man whom we'll henceforth refer to as "Coach K" of Duke almost always finishes first. Even when he loses, he wins. His fifth and last Army team posted a 9–17 mark, but instead of being fired (yes, they fire you at West Point too), he was named head coach of Duke.

"K" captained Bob Knight's 1968–1969 NIT team at The Point, coached for three years at the USMA Prep School in Fort Belvoir, Virginia, became Knight's first grad assistant at Indiana in 1972, and vaulted to the head coaching position at Army for five years until the Blue Devils beckoned in 1980. He coached two NIT teams at West Point, but really hit post-season pay dirt when his first major Duke recruits—Dawkins, Alarie, Henderson, Amaker, and Bilas—came of age. They gave a hint of what was in store when they closed out the 1985 season with a 23–8 log and a number ten national ranking. But 1985–1986 can best be described as "the stuff that dreams are made of": they won thirty-seven games (the most in NCAA history); claimed titles in the Big Apple NIT, ACC regular season, ACC Tournament, and the NCAA East Regionals; set a school record of a twenty-one game win skein; and, despite losing the NCAA championship game to Louisville by a single point, were voted the number one team in the land by the AP and UPI. After they captured the ACC Tourney title again in 1988, Coach K led his Blue Devils to the Final Four in Kansas City.

The New York Met hoop writers named Krzyzewski their Coach of the Year back in 1977. In 1984 Coach K assisted Bob Knight to the Olympic gold and was named the AP's ACC Coach of the Year, and in the "dream" season he was named national Coach of the Year by a nearly unanimous vote—and that's a lot more valuable than the Maltese falcon. During the summer of 1987, Krzyzewski took a select team of U.S. collegians to Yugoslavia for the World University Games.

*Coach K in Pittsburg, July 1986.*

Coach Mike Krzyzewski
Duke University
Durham, North Carolina

# 94. Shuffle and Slide Drill

A stifling man-for-man defense is at the core of Coach K's success and the accent of his two lively appearances at Five-Star.   One-player defensive drills for the motivated person are like the proverbial needle in a haystack, and the "Shuffle and Slide" is about the best there is.  Coach K includes many of the defensive moves needed to play legitimate pressure.  Remember, defending is an acquired skill that takes many hours of hard labor to master.  This drill is fantastic for the beginner, while the veteran can use it as a prime conditioner.  As Senator Bill Bradley (New York Knicks) once said, "When you're not practicing, someone else is.  Someday you'll meet that person and he'll beat you!"

1. Player stands under the basket in a defensive stance.  He shuffles up to the midpoint of the foul line.

2. Player then slides to his right until he reaches the end line.

3. Player then shuffles to the half court line.

4. Player then slides to his left until he reaches the opposite end line.

5. Player then shuffles backward until he reaches the foul line extended area.

6. Player then slides to his right until he reaches the foul lane.

7. Player then shuffles backward until he is out of bounds.

**Points of Emphasis:**

– Player should slide in his stance, keep his palms up, and avoid crossing his feet.

– When shuffling, the player should keep one hand up and the other hand down for balance.

– It is important that the player pick a point to focus his eyes on at all times.

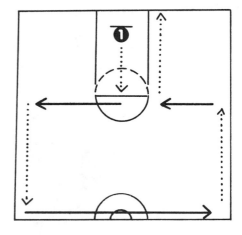

*Figure 94–1*

# Bob Knight

*Indiana University*

When Bob Knight left the friendly confines of West Point for the fast lane of Bloomington in 1971, some "experts" said he couldn't handle the quicker pace of the Big 10. He not only handled it, he remodeled it. Here's another "for instance": the Five-Star Basketball Camp. When he was hired as head coach in 1968 he demanded only one thing—that we implement a teaching mode incorporating "stations." Prior to this we had broken into teaching groups after lectures, but here was a way to showcase the remarkable talents of our coaches, each doing his thing, and to give campers a varied skill session each day. There are now sixteen of these stations going on simultaneously in a super-charged, ninety-minute morning period. Every camp and team in the United States worth its salt now uses stations in one form or another.

Knight watchers can recite chapter and verse about his brilliant accomplishments during his Indiana regime: three national championships (1976, 1981, 1987), Olympic and Pan-Am gold (1984 and 1979, respectively), an NIT title (1979), a Commissioner's Tourney crown (1974), eight Big 10 flags (five won outright), an astounding 468–169 (.735) won-lost lifetime mark, and somebody's Coach of the Year almost every time he posted. He's had best-selling teaching tapes, a controversial book, sold-out coaching clinics from coast to coast (including one-man spectaculars), and monumental press conferences. He's sent sixteen of his former assistants to NCAA head coaching jobs, and more are sure to follow. The Landon Turner Fund, established to aid his former player who was paralyzed in an automobile accident, is one of his many humanitarian ventures you don't read much about.

But with all of the above, we still like to dwell on his good old Army teams, those magnificent overachievers who amazed the hard-core hoop fans at the old and new Garden in New York. Talking about getting the most out of one's material, this was it. It was here, in the mid- to late 1960s, that Knight's hard-nosed defensive philosophy flourished and the beginnings of his Hoosier trademark, the motion offense, emerged. When you take the floor in post-season tournament play and never have the best player on the court, you've got to do something! Now the shoe is on the other foot, but whether the players are from West Point or Indiana, they still march to the beat of a single drummer—and you know who that is!

**Coach Bob Knight**
**Indiana University**
**Bloomington, Indiana**

# 95. Zigzag Drill

In July of 1987 Coach Knight began his twentieth year of association with Five-Star. He's demonstrated his "Zigzag" several times, and its basic simplicity coupled with the immense dividends derived from the drill never cease to amaze. You are practicing your defensive slides against an offensive ballhandler in a controlled situation. The proper fundamentals are stressed throughout the drill. Coach Knight is definitely not interested in having the dribbler "beat" the defender.

**Preparation:** Player #1 is a dribbler and player #2 is a defender. The court is divided invisibly down the middle and player #1 is not allowed to dribble across the invisible line.

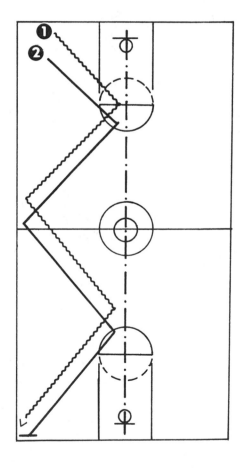

1. Player #1 dribbles the length of the court in a zigzag pattern.

2. Player #2, in his defensive stance, slides with the dribbler to the opposite end of the floor.

**Points of Emphasis:**

– The defensive player must always stand close enough to the offensive player so that he could put his palm on the offensive player's chest.

– The defensive player must keep his head directly between the ball and the basket.

– Players must apply constant pressure to the ball with their hands. The defensive player, playing palms up, pressures the ball with the hand nearest the direction the offensive player is moving. For example, if the offensive player moves to the right, the defensive player uses his right hand to flick the ball.

– Players should not cross their feet when moving or changing direction.

– If the offensive player turns his back on a reverse, the defensive player must retreat one step to avoid getting caught by the offensive step drop.

*Figure 95–1*

"The General" speaks: Bob Knight, then head coach at West Point, delivers his first lecture at Five-Star in 1968, at the old Rosemont site in Honesdale, Pennsylvania.

Co-director Howie Garfinkel presents Bob Knight with a plaque commemorating Knight's twenty-year association with Five-Star.

**Coach Bob Knight**
**Indiana University**
**Bloomington, Indiana**

# 96. Contesting the One-on-One Drill

Here is another great one from the "Dean of Defense." As we all know, most offenses start with a guard to wing pass. A good man-to-man defense wants to disrupt the natural flow of an opponent's offense. One of the main fundamentals of a good team "D" is to learn how to deny. Understanding the importance of this skill, Coach Knight has created a drill in which the defense must learn how to deny and open up to the ball effectively. He believes in giving the offense the advantage in order to make the defense work harder and eventually prevail. That's why the offense, when overplayed, can continually V cut to get open or go back door.

**Preparation:** Player #1 has the ball at the top of the key. Player #2 is the offensive player at the foul line extended area. Player #3 is the defensive player and stands in a total denial stance.

1. Player #2 V cuts back and forth as he tries to shake the defender (Figures 96–1 and 96–2).

2. If player #2 cannot get the ball, he cuts the baseline as player #3 opens up to see the ball (Figure 96–3).

**Points of Emphasis:**

– Player #3 must not let player #2 jump through the passing lane.

*Figure 96–1*

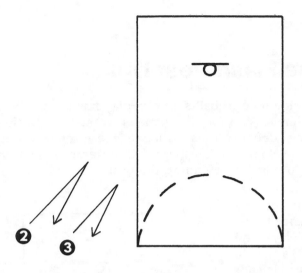

Figure 96–2

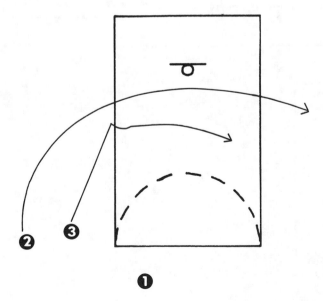

Figure 96–3

Coach Bob Knight
Indiana University
Bloomington, Indiana

# 97. Defending the Flash Post Drill

The transition from weak-side help to ball-side overplay has always been a tough assignment. The precise terminology in today's game is "rotation." In the lane area it could cost a bucket if the defense fails to make the proper adjustment or rotation. Coach Knight has developed an excellent drill to teach this concept and to give players the opportunity to practice defending the post.

**Preparation:** Player #1 has the ball and stands at the right foul line extended area. Player #2 is the other offensive player and stands at the left box. Player #3 stands in the lane in a help position and defends player #2.

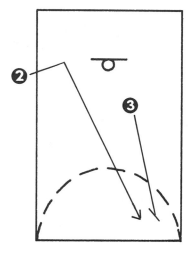

1. Player #2 V cuts to the high post on the ball side (Figures 97–1 and 97–3).

2. Player #3 must react and cut off player #2's passing lane (Figure 97–4).

3. Player #2 now spins and cuts to the low post ball side (Figure 95–2).

4. Player #3 must open up and properly defend the low post.

*Figure 97–1*

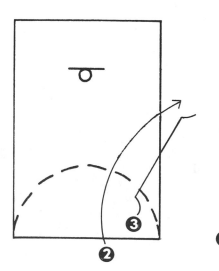

*Figure 97–2*

*Figure 97–3*

*Figure 97–4*

## Loren Wallace

*Bloomington High School*

If the walls of hallowed Lincoln Community High School could have their say, they'd tell us how Loren Wallace did it. The man definitely has a secret. Unfortunately we'll never know it, because he built a new empire at Bloomington, Illinois in the fall of 1987, and walls can't talk. But with only a handful of high Division I players over the past sixteen years—Chuck Verderber (Kentucky), Dan Duff (Notre Dame), and Joe Cook (you'll be hearing about him at Duke) are the most prominent—he left an unbeatable archive. Here are the highlights: a 361–89 career log, District Coach of the Year eight times, conference championships in twelve of his sixteen seasons, ten district titles, and a fourth place finish in the 1980 state tourney.

The answer to the riddle could be this: *defense!* No mystery, no magic, no mirrors. Regardless of the week he works Five-Star—and he's one of our top coaches since we moved to Robert Morris—he's our defensive guru. Pencil Wallace in for the "Big D" and go to sleep. Not so his pupils, who are wide awake to the cries of "Recover, hurry up, recover—you can't play defense behind the ball!" These words are also heard in every gym across the country.

*Loren Wallace demonstrating a footwork drill.*

Coach Loren Wallace
Bloomington High School
Bloomington, Illinois

# 98. Sprint Recovery Drill

When pressure is applied in a full court situation we lose our assignments, all too often, when our man passes the basketball. Coach Wallace has devised a full court drill to rectify this fault. The drill includes work on defensive slides, drop steps, and shuffles, ending with a little one-on-one fun before rotating positions.

**Preparation:** Player #1 and player #2 stand at the left corner, and player #3 stands at the mid-court area. Player #1 has the ball.

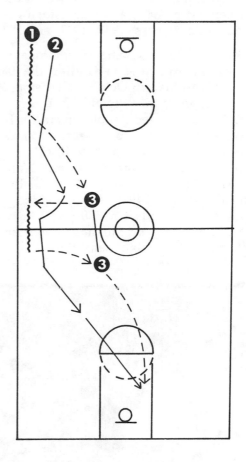

1. Player #1 starts a dribble advance up the court with player #2 guarding him.

2. Player #1 then throws the ball to player #3, forcing player #2 to retreat in the direction of the ball and ahead of it (proper position to help on penetrating move by the ball).

3. Player #3 returns the ball to player #1, thus requiring player #2 to recover to the ball.

4. Player #1 passes the ball back to player #3, again forcing player #2 to retreat to the help out position.

5. Player #3 throws the ball far down the court and player #2 sprints to retrieve it.

6. Players now rotate positions and repeat steps 1-5.

**Points of Emphasis:**

– This drill is designed to emphasize the fact that players should never play defense behind the ball.

*Figure 98–1*

# Gene Keady
*Purdue University*

Neither rain, nor sleet, nor hail, nor gloom of night (and that includes a storm-created power failure) could keep this courier from the swift completion of his Five-Star lecture. Even in the dark, Herb Sendek was able to salvage some of Gene Keady's dramatic defensive lecture for posterity. Coach Keady would not be stopped. It was as if he were back at Garden City J.C. (Kansas) rolling out from his All-American quarterback spot, or ripping through the line for the Pittsburgh Steelers, which he did briefly as a running back in 1958. Keady had been a three-sport star at Kansas State (football, baseball, and track). In 1966 he took over coaching duties at Hutchinson J.C. and remained until 1974. He won six league titles, took second place in the national tournament in 1973, and was named Junior College Coach of the Year from region six three straight years (1971, 1972, and 1973).

Keady made his name as a national recruiter under Eddie Sutton at Arkansas when he was instrumental in landing the famous Hog "Triplets"—Sidney Moncrief, Ron Brewer, and Marvin Delph. Next stop, Western Kentucky, as head coach. He guided the Hilltoppers into the NCAA Tourney in 1980, which also happened to be the year that Purdue needed a replacement for Lee Rose. In seven years as a Boilermaker he's never been out of a post-season tourney, has compiled five consecutive twenty-win seasons, has shared the Big 10 title in 1984 and 1987 (only out of the first division once), and earned the Big 10 and National Coach of the Year honors in 1984. This surprise club was picked to finish as low as ninth in the pre-season polls. His overall Purdue record is 149–65 (.698) and his lifetime head coaching ledger (including Beloit, Kansas H.S.) reads 475–178 (.727) in twenty-four years. There was a time when we considered this giant the most underrated coach in America, but the record proves he's just another overnight sensation.

*Just prior to the deluge that knocked out the lights and shrouded his lecture in semi-darkness, Gene Keady was talking up a storm of his own.*

Coach Gene Keady
Purdue University
Lafayette, Indiana

# 99. Clear Out Drill

The Gold and Black roster is dotted with Five-Star grads that include Troy Lewis, Todd Mitchell, Kip (Indiana) Jones, Tony Jones, Mel McCants, John Brugos, and Steve Scheffler, so Coach Keady and his staff are almost family. His "Clear Out Drill" is designed to teach the defensive player when to open up from his deny position and establish a help position. Coach goes further in stressing the importance of beating your man "to the spot." In Marv Kessler's Q & A lecture, one of the questions asked most often is "How and when do I open up to the ball from the wing?" We hope this drill answers that question.

**Preparation:** Player #1 has the ball and starts at mid-court. Player #2 is an offensive player and stands at the foul line extended midway between lane and end line. Player #3 is the defensive player in a deny position on player #2.

1. Player #1 dribbles toward player #2 (Figure 99–1).

2. Player #2 clears out as player #1 approaches.

3. Player #2 moves toward the baseline and cuts across the lane. Once on the other side of the lane, he flashes back in the post looking for a pass.

4. Player #3 maintains a good deny position until player #2 moves across the lane. Then player #3 opens up, enabling him to see both the ball and his man.

5. When player #2 flashes in the post, player #3 must recover and deny the pass (Figure 99–2).

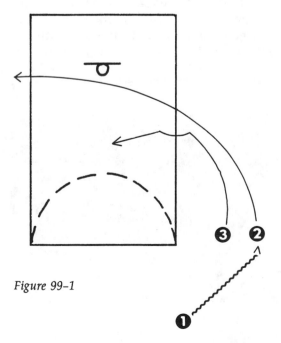

*Figure 99–1*

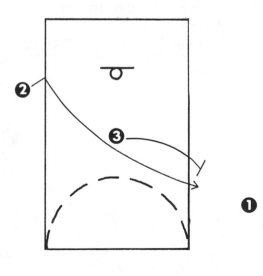

*Figure 99–2*

# Marv Kessler
*Washington Bullets*

For those who've heard Marv Kessler speak, no explanation is necessary. For those who haven't heard him, no explanation is possible. That's been the scenario for twenty-three years, and it will problably remain that way until teaching and good humor become passé. Fundamentally speaking, there is no one stronger in the game. And when you combine hilarity, pathos, and the very rudiments of the sport itself, it's no wonder that he has earned the tag, "The Poet of the Hardwood."

What would the camp and lecture circuit be—and particularly Five-Star—without the flying hair, the distinctive New York accent, the Jackie Masonish humor, and the nearly hour-long discourses (longer if you like) on the correct way to play "D," three-man, fast break, or you-name-it? Most of the you-name-its came from Individual Instruction, which he initiated in 1966. Moses Malone blocked his shots and the house came down, he held a high-level discussion with Isiah Thomas on the proper method to flick from behind without fouling, and he scorched the Dozier twins (Dunbar and South Carolina) with his famous "king-queen" routine. That's just a sample of the Kessler legacy, and there are hundreds of other examples.

"Lefty" came out of Boys High and learned from the master, Mickey Fisher. He was scholarshipped by Ev Case at N.C. State and, born to coach, he emerged in the early 1960s at Van Buren High in Queens, New York. Along with the Ron Johnsons (possibly the best guard in Five-Star history), Fosterbays, Edwards, Zimets, and the legendary "Shapiro," he battled the Mel Davis machine at Boys and those awesome DeWitt Clinton teams to near misses in the Public League playoffs. He was one of the last of the great PSAL coaches. In 1972 he took over an Adelphi College quint that had won eight games the previous year and proceeded to post a 17–9 mark. Spurred on by the tragic death of star forward Marshall Williams, his Panthers clawed their way into the 1977 NCAA Division II Tourney, only to turn down the bid at the last moment—an incredible story in itself. Marv joined Eddie Biedenbach at Davidson College in 1979–1980 and helped propel the Wildcats from last to first in one season. He has spent the last four years as an NBA scout, three with the Pistons and one with the Bullets. In July of 1987 he took a U.S. team to the Maccabi Pan-Am Games in Caracas, Venezuela.

*Marv Kessler and his first "Pro Division" Five-Star Championship team in 1966.*

Coach Marv Kessler
Washington Bullets
Washington, D.C.

# 100. Three-Man Take the Charge Drill

One of Coach Kessler's best bits in his "orgy of learning" is his stuff on taking the charge. Rotation to the ball defensively is being emphasized more and more in today's game. Part of rotating to the ball in the lane is being able to take an offensive charge effectively. If you never practice taking a charge, it's highly unlikely that you'll be able to execute the maneuver in a game situation. Remember, when you take a charge, bring it to the attention of the ref by falling down and grunting.

**Preparation:** Player #1 has the ball at the top of the key. Player #2 stands in the foul line extended area. Player #3 is a defensive player guarding a chair on the box.

1. Player #1 passes to player #2 and makes a V cut to the basket (give and go).

2. Player #3 makes an upswitch into the path of the dribbler (player #2). Player #3 must not switch too soon.

3. Upon impact, player #3 falls back and communicates to the official with a loud yell or grunt that contact has moved him.

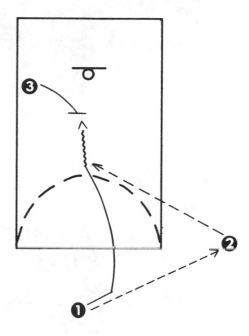

*Figure 100–1*

*A seance under the trees with one of Five-Star's all-time best, Marv Kessler.*

*Coach Kessler with Duke forward Ala Abdelnaby.*

Coach Marv Kessler
Washington Bullets
Washington, D.C.

# 101. Three-Man Take the Charge Versus Screen Drill

Teams are continuously screening for one another in today's game. The defender guarding the pick is usually drilled to hedge and recover on the ballhandler. Since a smart dribbler is aware of that, many times he will bust off the pick very quickly, knowing the hedge is used to make him slow up. Coach Kessler believes this is a great opportunity to step in and take the charge. Remember, it's the little things that distinguish the great players from the good ones.

**Preparation:** Player #1 has the ball on the side of the key. Player #2 is the other offensive player and stands at the foul line extended. Player #3 is the defensive player guarding player #2.

1. Player #2 comes up to set a screen on player #1's imaginary defender (Figures 101-1 and 101-2).

2. As player #1 comes off the screen with the dribble, player #3 upswitches into the path of player #1 and takes the charge (Figures 101-3 and 101-4).

3. Upon impact, player #3 falls back and communicates to the official with a loud yell or grunt that contact has moved him (Figures 101-5 and 101-6).

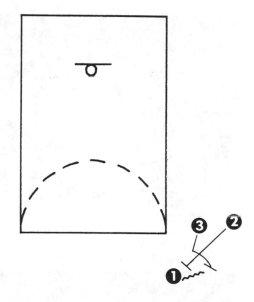

*Figure 101-1*

*Figure 101-2*

*Figure 101-3*

*Figure 101-4*

*Figure 101-5*

*Figure 101-6*

# Herb Sendek
*Providence College*

We once advised Herb Sendek, a 4.0 student at Carnegie-Mellon, to stay out of basketball. He was torn between a grad-assistantship at Providence and a $25,000-per-year trainee position in the business world. Despite moving up to full-time assistant in one year (the same route taken by "the mover," Rick Pitino), there's no question that Sendek could now be earning two to three times as much away from the hardwood. Were we right? Maybe yes, maybe no. The road to the Final Four is paved with opportunity!

Sendek claims he was not a natural student, so his burn-the-midnight-oil technique, nurtured at one of the finest seats of learning in the nation, fits perfectly into the Friars' scheme. But we wouldn't want his gas bill, then or now. To be an overachiever is one thing, but to be an overachiever and a perfectionist is an unbeatable combination for reaching one's potential. Herb Sendek's coaching star is on the rise.

*Five-Star has been stressing academics for more than twenty years. Herb Sendek, our academic guru, counsels rising freshmen and sophomores on how to get it done in the classroom.*

Coach Herb Sendek
Providence College
Providence, Rhode Island

# 102. Play the Ball, See the Man Drill

Sure, there are a lot of steps and teaching points in this drill, but Herb Sendek's invention, incorporated into the successful Providence practice program, is not as complex as it looks. You must change from one aspect of defensive positioning to another instantaneously—almost by rote. To become a top defender you must react quickly to a variety of situations, and this drill allows you to practice reacting to a series of defensive predicaments under actual game conditions. Only a 4.0 Carnegie-Mellon student would allow you to get into this maze!

**Preparation:** Player #1 stands at mid-court with the ball. Player #2 stands near player #1. Player #3 stands on the left foul line extended.

1. Player #1 takes three dribbles toward player #3 and stops his dribble (Figure 102–1).

2. Player #2 plays defense on player #1. When player #1 picks up his dribble, player #2 attacks him and yells "ball." Player #2 tries to deflect any pass without fouling.

3. Player #1 passes to player #3. At the same time, player #2 jumps to the ball side of player #1.

4. Player #1 now cuts to the basket, while player #2 maintains the ball-you-man position and prevents a pass to the cutter.

5. If player #1 does not get the ball, he proceeds to the weak side foul line extended (Diagram 102–2).

6. Player #2 stands so that he, the ball (player #3), and player #1 form a triangle. Player #2 should see both the ball and player #1 at all times (basic help position).

7. Player #3 dribbles hard to the baseline.

8. Player #2 plays the ball and cuts off player #3, using the baseline to help him.

9. Player #3 picks up his dribble as player #2 yells "ball" and tries for a deflection.

10. Player #3 passes to player #1, and player #2 pops to the middle to form a triangle again.

11. Player #1 drives to the basket to create a two-on-one situation (Figure 102–3).

12. Play continues until the offense scores or the defense stops them.

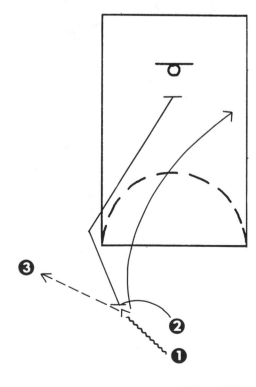

*Figure 102–1*

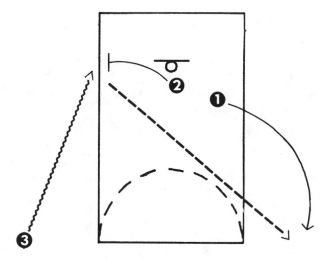

*Figure 102–2*

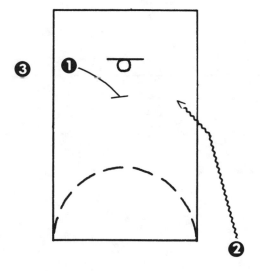

*Figure 102–3*

# PART EIGHT:

# BIG MAN DEVELOPMENT DRILLS

# Larry Brown

*Kansas University*

How Larry Brown ever got so good coming out of Long Beach, Long Island, a hotbed of surfers in the mid- to late 1950s, is one of the hoop mysteries of the century. He made his New York City debut in the livery of the New York Nationals, an "outside" team we coached in the 1950s and 1960s. No, we did not teach him how to play. He was a dandy from day one, and after leading the Nats to a few titles and graduating from Hargrave Military in Virginia, he entered North Carolina. The rest is, as we say, history: All-ACC 1962-1963, Olympic gold medal winner in 1964, MVP of the ABA's first All-Star game in 1967, then coach of the Carolina Cougars (ABA), Denver Nuggets (ABA-NBA), UCLA (runners-up to Louisville in 1980), New Jersey Nets (NBA), and coach at Kansas beginning in 1983. Brown, a teacher and a half, won two Big Eight Tourney crowns, made the NCAA post-season party every year he coached, and never won fewer than twenty games a season. In 1988 he took the Jayhawks to the Final Four in Kansas City, soaring to victory and winning his first NCAA Championship.

Coach Larry Brown
University of Kansas
Lawrence, Kansas

# 103. Dantley Drill

In most of the preceding chapters we've started you off with an easy drill and built up to the more complex ones. Here we're beginning tough because it's Larry Brown—and Kevin McHale and Adrian Dantley!

When Adrian Dantley was a 6'5'' sophomore at DeMatha High School, they said he was too small to play the pivot and too slow to move outside. He became an All-American. When "A.D." ventured to Notre Dame, they said he was still too small and slow to help the Irish. Using more moves than Flipper in deep, he once again confounded the experts. Adrian is still 6'5'', still slow end-to-end, and still taking his man inside. Only now he's doing it for the NBA Pistons and "they" retired years ago when Dantley was named All-Pro.

What are the contributing factors to Dantley's remarkable success, other than his heart? Quickness, timing, touch, strength, and confidence. All but touch are covered in Coach Brown's drill. Dantley has owned that since birth.

**Preparation:** Player stands on the left side of the basket.

1. Player faces the backboard and holds the ball above his head (Figure 103–1).

2. Player jumps as high as he can and pounds the ball on the backboard without releasing it (Figure 103–2).

3. Player comes back down to the floor, quickly jumps back up, and performs a layup (Figures 103–3, 103–4).

4. Player rebounds the ball out of the net, slides to the right side of the backboard, and repeats steps 1–3 from the right side.

5. Player performs steps 1–4 until he makes ten baskets, five from each side.

**Points of Emphasis:**

– The drill should be performed three times.

– Player should concentrate on putting the ball against the backboard forcefully and going up for the shot quickly.

*Figure 103–1*

*Figure 103–2*

*Figure 103–3*

*Figure 103–4*

Coach Larry Brown
University of Kansas
Lawrence, Kansas

# 104. McHale Drill

Parts of Coach Brown's "Summer Improvement" clinics at Five-Star featured the McHale-Dantley expositions. Kevin McHale is flat-out one of the greatest power-forwards of all time. But it wasn't always so. Larry named this drill after the super Celt to emphasize some of his unique talents, like fabulous hands, timing, eye-hand coordination, and jumping consistency. This is a difficult drill for the advancing big guy, but if you can conquer "The McHale Drill," you can conquer anything!

**Preparation:** Player stands on the left side of the basket.

1. Player tosses the ball off the backboard.

2. Player jumps high and taps the ball with his left hand while tapping the rim with his right hand.

3. Player taps the ball eleven times, tapping the ball into the basket on the eleventh tap.

4. Player moves to the right side of the basket and performs steps 1–3, this time tapping the ball with his right hand while tapping the rim with his left hand.

**Points of Emphasis:**

– The drill should be performed three times.

*Dean Smith of North Carolina during a shooting lecture and demonstration in Honesdale.*

# Seth Greenberg

*California State University at Long Beach*

No, it's not quite true that the Greenberg brothers, Seth and Brad, have been dribbling at Five-Star since birth. It just seems that way. Seth has been "Mr. Dependable" for eighteen years: camper, counselor, resident coach, stationmaster, Staff Day speaker, commissioner, and Morning Mini-Lecture entrepreneur. Five-Star has always run most smoothly when the Greenberg brothers were at the throttle. They are to dedication and organization what Horowitz is to the keyboard.

Seth played at Fairleigh Dickinson in New Jersey under the great Al LoBalbo (now an assistant at St. John's) and began his coaching career immediately thereafter as a full-time assistant at Columbia. Before moving to Miami of Florida he recruited some heavy hitters for Pittsburgh (the fruits of his labors are still apparent) and volunteered at Virginia for a year. Tito Horford's remarkable improvement for the 'Canes can be traced directly to the many hours he and Coach Greenberg spent on the hardwood floor. Right after the 1987 season concluded, Seth accepted an offer from Cal State Long Beach that he couldn't refuse—associate coach with "Godfather" Joe Harrington (formerly of George Mason).

**Coach Seth Greenberg**
**California State University at Long Beach**
**Long Beach, California**

# 105. Taps Drill

In the development of the Horford types, offensive rebounding is a primary concern. "Paint people" must be able to convert a missed shot into a bucket as quickly as possible. Coach Greenberg is developing consistent leaping ability, hands, timing, and the instinct for keeping the ball alive. One of the classic drills!

**Preparation:** Player stands on the right side of the basket.

1. Player tosses the ball off the backboard.

2. With his right hand player taps the ball off the lower part of the backboard, concentrating on quick jumps.

3. The player taps the ball a total of eleven times, tapping the ball into the basket on the eleventh tap.

4. Player repeats the drill from the left side of the basket, using his left hand.

**Points of Emphasis:**

– The drill should be performed three times.

*From Punxsutawney to the pros: Chuck Daly, after his 1968 Honesdale lecture, was not too busy to lend a hand at a follow-up station. Daly, then the new Boston College head coach, is now the NBA's most underrated mentor with the Detroit Pistons.*

Coach Seth Greenberg
California State University at Long Beach
Long Beach, California

# 106. Rim Touching Drill

Every year players are reaching new heights with their jumping ability. There are numerous "slam dunk" contests everywhere which have yet to prove anything. Unfortunately, most of the super leapers can only achieve their elevation off a running start. How many times in a game are you able to get an uncontested running start?

In the "Rim Touching Drill" Coach Greenberg teaches the importance of becoming a consistent leaper from a standing position. This drill should help increase your jump, stamina, leg power, and conditioning.

**Preparation:** Player stands directly in front of the basket.

1. Player extends his right arm and locks his elbow.

2. Player taps the rim of the basket with his right hand ten times, bouncing after each tap without taking a step.

3. Player repeats steps 1–2 using his left hand.

4. Player repeats steps 1–2 using both hands.

**Points of Emphasis:**

– The drill should be performed three times.

**Coach Bill Aberer**
**La Salle Academy**
**New York, New York**

# 107. Mikan Drill

Voted the Player of the First Half Century and certainly the most colorful "giant" of the early era of basketball was DePaul's and the Minneapolis Lakers' George Mikan. But "Big George," who weighed a massive 240 pounds and stood 6'9'', towering over most of his opposition save 7'0'' Bob (Foothills) Kurland of Okhahoma A & M (now Oklahoma State), was not always an outstanding player. As a matter of fact, Mikan was somewhat clumsy and awkward when he arrived at DePaul. The coaching staff developed a series of drills to improve his coordination and stamina. They helped make him a dominant force under the hoop. Over the years these widely used exercises have been dubbed the "Mikan Drills," although they probably should be called the "Ray Meyer Drills" after their inventor, the "Hall of Fame" coach of DePaul.

Coach Aberer, who has taught this series many times at Five-Star, stresses a few very important points: 1) keep your arms extended over your head at all times, 2) use your right hand on the right side of the basket and your left hand on the left side to shoot, and 3) jump to your peak every time.

**Preparation:** Player stands on the right side of the basket in the three-second lane as shown in Figure 107-1.

1. Player holds the ball over his head with his arms extended and his elbows locked (Figure 107-2).

2. Player jumps and scores a layup off the backboard, using his right hand to shoot.

3. Player immediately takes a step under the basket and rebounds the ball with both hands over his head, grasping the ball while it is still in the net.

4. Player takes a step to the left side of the basket and repeats the drill, using his left hand to shoot (Figure 107-3).

5. Player repeats steps 1-4 until he makes ten baskets, five from each side.

**Points of Emphasis:**

- The drill should be performed three times.

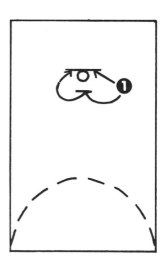

*Figure 107-1*

*Figure 107–2*

*Figure 107–3*

# Tom McCorry
*James Madison University*

Tom McCorry had it figured right. Take the greatest senior in Five-Star history, romp over eleven beleaguered foes in a row, collect your gold, and then quit. Let's face it, can you top going undefeated with Moses Malone? That was in August 1973, and "The McCorry," who was elevated to head coach following his Malone caper, is still on the job. Needless to say, his sessions are marvels of organization and discipline. It's interesting to note that one of Tom's first pupils in his initial head coaching position at St. Dominic's High School was Rick Pitino. But the "main dude" was Tom Riker (South Carolina All-American), whom he developed into one of the finest men in Long Island annals. After switching to Xavier (NYC) High School, he coached the Catholic All-Stars in the first annual "City Game" in 1970 (Brian Winters, Ed Searcy, Jap Trimble, Len Elmore, and John Ryan). The Publics won, however, 100–99 (Greg McDougald, Bernard Hardin, Tom Henderson, Dave Edwards, and Howie Robertson).

While staying put at Five-Star for twenty years, the ubiquitous McCorry—obviously in demand—won assistant coaching jobs at Fairfield, Boston College, Boston University, and Northeastern, and helped James Madison off the deck and into the NIT in 1986–1987. His work with big men, in or out of Five-Star, is extraordinary. No one does a better job of teaching the fundamentals to the big folks.

*Moses Malone, in his last game at Five-Star, leads his team to the championship under coach Tom McCorry.*

*From Moses to Mourning: Coach McCorry instructing high school Player of the Year Alonzo Mourning.*

Coach Tom McCorry
James Madison University
Harrisonburg, Virginia

# 108. Drop Step Moves

One of the essential moves a big guy must acquire is the drop step. In this drill Coach McCorry develops the routine of ball faking, sealing, proper body balance, and power dribble technique. An aside to all you big people: The shorter players have their three-point shot, but you're saddled with the old-fashioned deuce. Make your coach want to go to you! The way to accomplish this goal is to master the moves on this and subsequent pages.

**Preparation:** Player stands underneath the basket.

1. Player spins the ball out to position A (right box), B (left box), C (right lane midpoint), or D (left lane midpoint) in Figure 108–1.

2. Player chases the ball, catches the ball, and comes to a jump stop with his body well balanced, buttocks down (Figures 108–2 and 108–3).

3. Player ball fakes over his shoulder without moving his feet, and then executes a drop step power move to the basket (Figure 108–4). (If player ball fakes to the middle area, he drops the foot nearest the baseline in such a way as to seal off his defender. He then makes one power dribble, keeping the ball between his legs, squares up to the backboard, and makes a power layup [Figure 108–5].)

4. Steps 1–3 should be repeated with fakes to the remaining positions.

**Points of Emphasis:**

– The drill should be done quickly for three minutes.

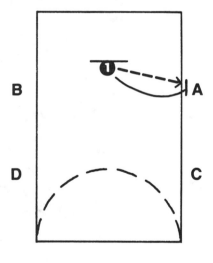

*Figure 108–1*

*Figure 108–2*

*Figure 108–3*

*Figure 108–4*

*Figure 108–5*

Coach Tom McCorry
James Madison University
Harrisonburg, Virginia

# 109. Ball Roll Drill

In this drill Coach McCorry is trying to develop an important tool that every big man should possess: the head and shoulders fake. Coach McCorry insists that when the player uses the head and shoulders fake, he should fake outward from his chest instead of from straight above his head. By mastering this move the big man will be able to get his shot off in traffic much more easily. Also, the likelihood of drawing a foul from the defender is greater.

**Preparation:** Player stands at the right elbow.

1. Player rolls the ball toward the near box.

2. Player follows the ball, picks it up, squares up to the backboard, pump fakes, and scores a power layup or dunk.

3. Player repeats steps 1–2 from the left elbow.

4. Player continues until he makes twenty baskets, ten from each side.

**Points of Emphasis:**

- The drill should be performed three times.

- The pump fake should not be done over the player's head, but at an angle out from his chest.

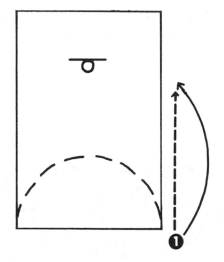

*Figure 109–1*

Coach Tom McCorry
James Madison University
Harrisonburg, Virginia

# 110. Jump Shot Drill

Here's one of the simplest yet best organized drills to improve the jump shooting ability of the center and power-forward—or even the very young backcourt and wing player. It's important that the big people concentrate on form and technique rather than on speed. The great players use the backboard as deliciously as Hershey uses chocolate, so "go glass" from spots A-B-C-D. However, on shots from areas C and D that are taken turning to the middle, "go swish."

**Preparation:** Player starts at position A (right box) in Figure 110-1.

1. Player shoots ten consecutive jump shots. The player follows each shot, and if he misses a shot he must rebound, square up to the backboard, and score.

2. Player takes ten shots at each remaining position, proceeding in this order: position B (left box), position C (right lane midpoint), position D (left lane midpoint), position E (right elbow), position F (left elbow), position G (right baseline step-out area), position H (left baseline step-out area), and position I (foul line midpoint).

*Figure 110-1*

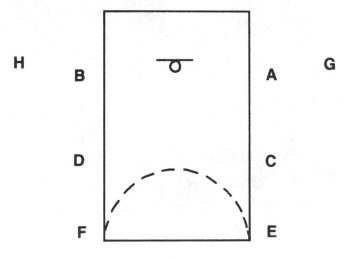

# Brendan Malone

*New York Knicks*

To quote Hubie Brown, Brendan Malone does "as good a job scouting opponents as I've ever seen." Considering that Brown's disciples include Mike Fratello, Rick Pitino, Stan Albeck, Richie Adubato, and Frank Layden, that's high praise indeed. So now we know Malone "sees" the game. What we've been dead sure about for fifteen years is that he can coach it and teach it. Trent Tucker, the Knicks' fine shooting guard, lends this evidence: "Brendan really relates well to players." There's nothing left, folks, Malone's the goods!

In six years at famed Power Memorial, home of Kareem Abdul-Jabbar (Lew Alcindor for the nonbelievers) and Lenny Elmore, Malone won two New York City Catholic titles plus a JV crown the first year. He joined the Five-Star family in 1974 and has been there every year since, the last five as master of Station 13 and the Morning Mini-Lecture, a job which can tax the ingenuity and endurance of a Kissinger. His drills for players of all ages and abilities are models of clarity and organization. And that's how he teaches, whether it be to a fifteen-year-old sophomore or a hardened NBA veteran.

Brendan went the college route in 1976 with Fordham, tried Yale the following year, spent six seasons as Jim Boeheim's first assistant, and took the head job at Rhode Island in 1984. Hubie called in 1986, and the combination of working with that all-timer coupled with the mystique of the pros proved irresistible. He was rehired by the Knicks in the summer of 1987.

*We can just hear Brendan Malone advising, "say goodbye to your basketball."*

Coach Brendan Malone
New York Knicks
New York, New York

# 111. Duck-In Move Drill

A relatively new term in basketball, the "duck-in" was called "posting up" ten years ago. This drill is designed to get the pass to the big man in the paint. We are teaching the pivot man the following: 1) to position himself properly in the paint, 2) to help create a passing lane and thereby decrease the degree of difficulty for the passer, 3) to catch the ball under pressure, 4) three offensive moves once he has received the pass, and 5) the most important part of all: "to read your defender!"

**Preparation:** Player #1 has the ball and stands at the top of the key on the left side. Player #2 stands to the right of the lane. Player #3 stands in the lane. Player #2 is the offensive big man and player #3 is the defensive player.

1. Player #2 brings his defensive man (player #3) into the lane. He must break the broken circle to do this. If possible, he should line himself up so that he is in front of the rim.

2. Player #3 stays with player #2 and contests the passing lane.

3. When player #2 reaches the broken circle he ducks down low. Then he hits the elbow of the defender so that it flies upward, creating a lane for the pass. Player #2 now shows his free hand and calls for the ball.

4. Player #2 can now execute one of three offensive moves depending on how the defensive player reacts: 1) If the defender does not react well, player #2 executes a drop step and a horse dribble (a dribble between his legs), and then he squares up to lay up the ball. 2) If the defender reacts and recovers, player #2 takes one dribble toward the box, and then he takes two steps and executes a baby hook. 3) If the defender recovers and positions himself between player #2 and the basket, player #2 drop steps, horse dribbles, squares up and uses a head and shoulders pump fake, and then he goes strong to the defender and scores.

**Points of Emphasis:**

– If player #2 uses a head and shoulders pump fake, he should not fake the ball up, but instead should fake it out of his chest to elevate the defender.

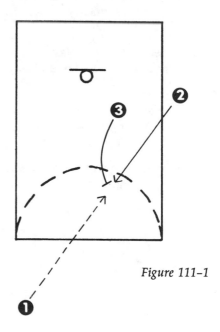

*Figure 111–1*

Coach Brendan Malone
New York Knicks
New York, New York

# 112. Power Shot Drill

Many of the aforementioned fundamentals are in this drill: the jump stop, the ball fake, the footwork pivot, the ability to square to the hole, and the basic shot itself. The V cut and the offensive stick back are also stressed. It's non-stop action, and fatique is definitely a factor in this one-minute "ordeal."

**Preparation:** One ball is placed on each of the boxes. Player #1 stands behind the basket out of bounds.   Player #2 and player #3 position themselves in the lane near the broken circle.

1.  Player #1 runs out to the box on the left side, jump stops, picks up the ball, ball fakes to the middle, pivots, squares up to the basket, and shoots a short bank shot (Figures 112-1, 112-2, 112-3, 112-4).

2.  After the shot attempt, player #1 runs underneath the basket, V cuts up to the box on the right side, and repeats the sequence in step 1. It is important that he not watch the ball after he shoots but moves quickly to the other side to get another shot off.

3.  After each shot, player #2 or player #3 rebounds the ball and places it back on the box.

4.  Player #1 continues the drill for one minute, trying to get off as many shots as possible.

5.  Player #2 and player #3 take turns performing the drill.

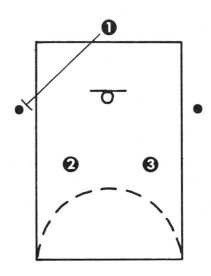

*Figure 112-1*

*Figure 112–2*

*Figure 112–3*

*Figure 112–4*

*1986 NBA Coach of the Year Mike Fratello demonstates the "duck-in" move for some aspiring pros.*

# Dave Odom
*University of Virginia*

The Old South, as Margaret Mitchell once put it, is "Gone with the Wind," but much of its charm remains packaged in the personality of G. David Odom. The good ol' country boy from Goldsboro, North Carolina, has triumphed over the most difficult chore in coaching—being an equally gifted first and second banana. After playing a mean backcourt for Guilford College, Odom opted for teaching and coaching at Durham Senior High School, where he ran the show like a Tony winner. Next stop, Wake Forest. Under Carl Tacy, and firmly supported by Odom's recruits, the Deacons reached the NCAA Final Eight in 1976, were an ACC Tourney finalist in 1977 (lost to the Spanarkel-Gminski group), and won twenty games in 1978. Among his most notable finds were Frank Johnson (now Bullets), Jim Johnstone, Alvis Rogers, and Guy Morgan.

Odom left in 1979 for the top banana spot at East Carolina. It was a delicious season for the Pirates, who earned their first winning campaign in nine years. G. David remained until 1982 when Terry Holland called from Virginia. The "Gentleman Coach" needed a right hand, and Odom's is among the firmest in the business. His lack of ego is also legend, so Odom paddled back to the mainstream. The Cavaliers have enjoyed post-season play in all the years of his tenure.

The biggest move Five-Star ever made was to Wheeling, West Virginia in 1975. Paul Baker, then head coach of Wheeling College, brought us, but Dave Odom, in his final year at Durham High, brought the sunshine—and some players. Hired over the phone at the suggestion of Penn coach Chuck Daly, currently knocking 'em dead with the Detroit Pistons, Odom was "Mr. Versatility"—a spirited coach, flawless station-master, crafty recruiter, and a bridge between the north and south for Klein and Garfinkel. He was the natural choice to be head coach at Robert Morris College when the camp outgrew the Wheeling facility. He was the unofficial aide to Fratello and took over in 1979. He's been head coach there ever since and serves in the same capacity in Radford, Virginia. Odom also runs the Five-Star Women's Camp at Radford in mid-June.

**Coach Dave Odom**
**University of Virginia**
**Charlottesville, Virginia**

# 113. Power Layup Drill

In the "Power Layup Drill," Coach Odom has created a typical game situation to improve the big man's ability to score in traffic. Making the drill even more realistic, the defenders are allowed to bump or harass the big man on the shot attempt—a real "blue collar rumble."

**Preparation:** Player #1 stands on the foul line. Player #2 and player #3 surround the ball in the lane (Figure 113–1).

1. Player #2 and player #3 extend their arms in an umbrella fashion (Figure 113–2).

2. Player #3 claps his hands twice.

3. Player #1 sprints to the ball and picks it up, bringing it to a strong chin position (Figure 113–3).

4. Player #2 and player #3 provide resistance with their arms and bodies.

5. Player #1 powers up and through the defenders' arms. The defenders should not jump to block the shot, but they may foul with their bodies or arms (Figure 113–4).

6. After the shot is made, player #1 sprints back to the foul line and repeats steps 1–5 two times.

**Points of Emphasis:**

– Each player performs the drill three times.

*The Rainmaker? No, Dave Odom is not praying for rain. The Virginia Cavalier assistant and Five-Star head coach is "bellying up to the shooter" in a defensive lecture in Pittsburgh.*

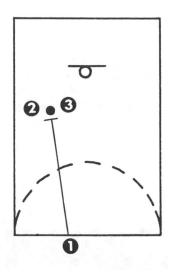

*Figure 113–1*

*Figure 113–2*

*Figure 113–3*

*Figure 113–4*

# Rick Albro
*East Grand Rapids High School*

Two things are guaranteed to happen when Rick Albro comes to Five-Star. He's going to complete a great week of coaching and comraderie, and he'll lose his voice before his Staff Day lecture. But the big guy toughs it out, and the kids learn what it takes to play in the "pits." This tireless technician developed Garde Thompson for Michigan; Jim Boylan, a 20+ scorer, for Maine; and 6'3" major-leaguer-to-be Joe Middleton, among others. His East Grand Rapids teams are always competitive and models of decorum.

*Rick Albro shows box-out technique. Fess Irvin, high school All-American and later a Louisiana State University star, stands at the far left. Next to him (holding a basketball) is Lloyd Daniels, who is, according to Garf, "Magic Johnson with a legitimate jump shot"—and one of the best players to attend Five-Star.*

Coach Rick Albro
East Grand Rapids High School
East Grand Rapids, Michigan

# 114. Twenty-One Taps Drill

Coach Albro's rebounding and/or back-to-basket moves stations are always fast-moving and vigorous. Here he takes a popular schoolyard game and turns it into an inventive teaching situation. One player is practicing his free throw accuracy under pressure while the other two have the opportunity to improve their ability to tap in a missed shot. It's fun and games while building confidence at the charity stripe.

**Preparation:** Player #1 has the ball and stands on the free throw line in front of the basket. Player #2 and player #3 stand on the boxes opposite one another.

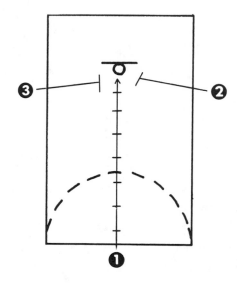

1. Player #1 shoots a free throw. If he makes a basket, he scores one point, retains possession of the ball, and makes another attempt. If he misses the basket, player #2 and player #3 have the opportunity to tap the ball in the basket. A basket scored off a tap counts as two points and gives the player the right to go to the free throw line.

2. If a player makes three free throws in a row, he automatically rotates to one of the boxes.

3. If a player misses a free throw and the other two players miss the tap, the player shooting from the free throw line retains his position there.

*Figure 114-1*

4. Play continues until one player scores twenty-one points.

# PART NINE:

# BASKETBALL SMORGASBORD

Coach Hubie Brown
CBS-TV

# Two-Minute Box Drills

The four Hubie Brown "Box Drills," developed during his run with Atlanta, have been a staple with the Hawks, Knicks, and Five-Star campers for several years.  Two players should work together alternately on each drill.  The pros go through the routine effortlessly, but we can tell you you'll not do these at the proper tempo in thirty seconds apiece right off the bat.  It will take time, patience, and concentration to master this torrent of fundamentals.  You'll learn how to "pick and roll" with expertise, play "one-on-one" the right way, "give and go" like the book says, and "block the shot" without fouling.

# 115. Pick and Roll

**Preparation:**   Player #1 and player #2 stand at the points where the lane lines meet the baseline.  Player #1 has the ball.

1.  Player #1 rolls the ball diagonally across the key (Figure 115-1).

2.  Player #1 follows the ball, gets behind the ball and picks it up, faces the basket with his eyes on the rim, and stands in a triple threat position.

3.  Player #2 crosses the lane and touches the box, then goes to the elbow opposite the ball and receives a chest pass from player #1 (Figure 115-2).

4.  Player #1 follows his pass and sets a screen for player #2 who fakes to his left to set up player #1.

5.  Player #2 then takes two dribbles past player #1's screen.  Player #1 pivots on his inside foot, opens to the ball, and seals out an imaginary defender.

6.  Player #2 may take a jump shot, drive the lane, or pass to player #1 on his roll to the hoop.  If player #1 receives the ball, he takes a shot.

7.  The player who does not attempt a shot follows for the rebound.

*Figure 115-1*

*Figure 115-2*

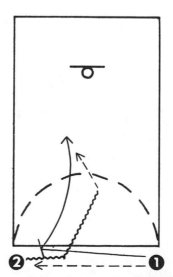

**Coach Hubie Brown**
**CBS-TV**

# 116. One-on-One

**Preparation:** Player #1 and player #2 stand at the points where the lane lines meet the baseline. Player #1 has the ball.

1. Player #1 rolls the ball diagonally across the key.

2. Player #1 follows the ball, gets behind the ball and picks it up, faces the basket with his eyes on the rim, and stands in a triple threat position.

3. Player #2 crosses the lane and touches the box, and then goes diagonally across the key to play defense on player #1.

4. Player #2 puts his hand on player #1's hip and the players begin one-on-one play.

5. The offensive player may not dribble more than three times before he shoots. A missed field goal attempt puts both players into a scramble for the loose ball and play begins again. The drill ends when one of the players makes a basket.

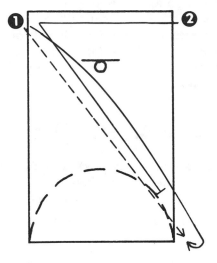

*Figure 116–1*

Coach Hubie Brown
CBS-TV

# 117. Give and Go

**Preparation:** Player #1 and player #2 stand at the points where the lane lines meet the baseline. Player #1 has the ball.

1. Player #1 rolls the ball diagonally across the key (Figure 117–1).

2. Player #1 follows the ball, gets behind the ball and picks it up, faces the basket with his eyes on the rim, and stands in a triple threat position.

3. Player #2 crosses the lane and touches the box.

4. Player #2 goes to the elbow opposite the ball and receives a chest pass from player #1 (Figure 117–2).

5. Player #1 fakes right, pushes off his right foot, and cuts inside player #2 in a straight line to the basket.

6. Player #2 makes a bounce pass to player #1.

7. Player #1 shoots a layup.

8. Player #2 follows his pass. He either rebounds player #1's missed shot and scores, or he takes the ball out of the net and repeats the drill.

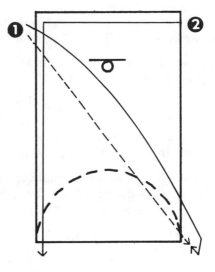

*Figure 117–1*

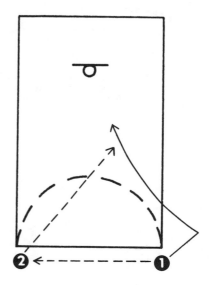

*Figure 117–2*

Coach Hubie Brown
CBS-TV

# 118. Block the Shot

**Preparation:**   Player #1 and player #2 stand at the points where the lane lines meet the baseline.  Player #1 has the ball.

1. Player #1 rolls the ball diagonally across the key (Figure 118–1).

2. Player #1 follows the ball, gets behind the ball and picks it up, faces the basket with his eyes on the rim, and stands in a triple threat position.

3. Player #2 crosses the lane and touches the box and then goes to the elbow opposite the ball.

4. Player #1 fakes a shot and drives to the hoop (Figure 118–2).

5. Player #2 cuts across the key diagonally to block player #1's shot, using his inside hand to avoid a foul.

6. If the shot is missed or blocked, player #2 must retrieve the ball and score.

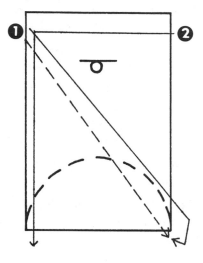

*Figure 118–1*

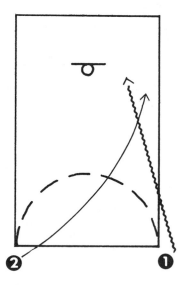

*Figure 118–2*

*The first Hubie Brown demonstration at Five-Star.*

# Will Rey
*University of Evansville*

It's quite a sight to see Will Rey in action, especially when he's preaching his "Cone Drills." The orange cones are glistening, the Mikasa balls are thumping, and behind all the cosmetics is a coach of considerable depth and sincerity. The former señor of Chicago's Fenwick and Crete-Monee High Schools was recommended to Five-Star nine years ago by Jerry Wainwright. Coach Rey, in turn, sent two fine Chicago mentors, Carl Costello (Crete-Monee) and Paul Pryma (St. Ignatius)—and the Windy City beat goes on. In 1985 Will joined Bob Knight disciple Jim Crews at Evansville, of the Midwestern Collegiate Conference. The Purple Aces took off in 1987 and copped the regular season championship.

Rey is a tremendous teacher—he has a total grasp of fundamentals, and he can organize and articulate any topic with complete respect for the audience. A star of Staff Day, Rey made his Five-Star Station 13 debut at Radford in June of 1987.

Coach Will Rey
University of Evansville
Evansville, Indiana

# Dribbling Drills

The following dribbling drills and dribble moves must be mastered by any individual wishing to develop into a complete player. The proficient dribbler is able to: 1) face the defense and see the entire floor, 2) eliminate the overly aggressive defender, and 3) back up in traffic and maintain poise. This program is designed to develop these three skills. Each player needs only a ball, an open playing surface, and a tremendous desire to improve his dribbling ability.

## General Components

The dribbler should assume a good balanced body position: head up, chin parallel to the ground, feet shoulder width apart, and knees bent to keep the body low. The fingers of the dribble hand should be spread comfortably with the hand slightly cupped as this affords good ball control. The wrist of the dribble hand does the majority of the work and the elbow of the dribble arm is kept close to the body in an effort to eliminate upper arm motion. The dribble itself should be kept low, no higher than mid-thigh, and should hit the floor in front and slightly outside of the feet. The ball should be dribbled hard—the harder the dribble, the quicker the ball returns to the hand, and the quicker the dribbler can move.

## Stationary Lead-Up Drills

The player executes these five drills as he stands in place in a low, balanced position with his feet parallel. The purpose of these exercises is to develop the hand movement necessary to master the actual dribble moves.

1. **Side to Side:** The player dribbles the ball in a V fashion in front of his body, moving his hand from one side to the other as quickly as possible. He should perform this first with his weak hand and then with his strong hand.

2. **Push and Pull:** The player dribbles the ball in a V fashion on the side of his body, moving his hand from the front to the back of the ball so that the ball is actually pushed forward and pulled backward. The player should perform this first with his weak hand and then with his strong hand.

3. **Hand to Hand:** The player dribbles the ball in a V fashion from hand to hand as quickly as possible. The player should perform this first in front of his body and then behind his body.

4. **Figure Eight:** The player dribbles the ball in a figure eight fashion around both his legs using his right and left hands. Initially he dribbles the ball through his legs from back to front, then he changes directions and dribbles from front to back.

5. **Two Balls:** With a ball in each hand, the player begins with a quick, hard dribble just outside and in front of his feet. The balls should be dribbled no higher than

the knees. Then the player uses the same push and pull drill move described in number 2 above. Having a ball in each hand increases the difficulty of this maneuver. The player brings the balls back to their original starting positions, resumes the quick, hard dribble, and changes hands by crossing the balls over. The player concludes this routine by handling the two balls in a random fashion, i.e., dribbling between and around his legs or changing hands.

# Dribble Moves

The dribbler should attempt to learn these five change of direction moves. Mastering these is important because basketball is a game of angles.

1. **Front Crossover:** The dribbler plants the foot corresponding with the dribble hand and steps with his opposite foot in the direction he wishes to go. He pushes off and explodes off his planted foot. He pushes the ball over to his other hand in a V fashion in front of him as his foot is planted. His dribble hand is moved from the top to the side of the ball with the fingers pointed toward the floor. As the dribbler improves, he can add a head fake as the foot is planted.

2. **Between the Legs:** The dribbler stands with the foot opposite his dribble hand in front of him, with the weight of his body on this foot. He pushes back through his extended leg to his other hand. Again, his dribble hand is on the side of the ball with the fingers pointed toward the floor. The move is completed by bringing the back leg up and over to protect the ball.

3. **Behind the Back:** As in the front crossover move, the dribbler plants the foot corresponding with the dribble hand and steps with his opposite foot. As he plants and pushes off, he moves his dribble hand to the side of the ball and points his fingers toward the floor, and the ball is pushed behind his back and forward ahead of his body. The dribble hand is extended as far as possible behind his back.

4. **Pullback Crossover:** The dribbler moves the foot opposite his dribble hand forward and moves his body sideways into a protective stance with his non-dribble arm up and parallel to the floor. He comes to a momentary stop while maintaining his dribble. The dribbler then pulls back two full dribbles and slide steps in order to stay in a protective stance. He moves his dribble hand from the top to the front of the ball and points his fingers toward the floor. Once the pullback is completed, he plants his back foot and executes a front crossover move as described above.

5. **In and Out:** This move is essentially a counter to the front crossover. The ball is kept in the same hand throughout this entire move. As the dribbler approaches the defense, he steps with the foot opposite the dribble hand as if he were going to change direction. He moves his dribble hand to the side of the ball and begins a crossover dribble. The ball and his foot should hit the floor simultaneously. Then the dribbler immediately moves his dribble hand to the opposite side, brings the ball back to his side, and makes a strong push off his extended foot as he continues in his original path. As he becomes proficient, he can add a head and shoulders fake.

Coach Will Rey
University of Evansville
Evansville, Indiana

# 119. One-on-One Cone Drill Number One

Coach Rey's "Cone Drills" are marvels of simplicity and cover nearly every facet of individual offense. The cones (or chairs) simulate defenders, and the drill can be performed by one, two, or any number of players. The only question is, how bad do you want to be good?

**Preparation:** Cones are placed just inside the free throw circle sixteen feet from the baseline. Player #1 and player #2 stand at the points where the lane lines meet the baseline. Each player has a ball.

1. Player #1 begins by executing a proper strong side or crossover start and dribbles with his right hand from the baseline to the outside of the cone. Once he is past the cone, he jump stops and pivots on his left foot to square to the basket.

2. At this point player #1 executes five moves: 1) a jab step and a jump shot, 2) a jump shot fake, a strongside move, one dribble with the right hand across the face of the basket, and a layup on the right side, 3) a jump shot fake, a crossover move, one dribble with the left hand, and a layup from the left side, 4) a jump shot fake, a big dribble with the right hand, and a pullup jump shot from the dotted line, 5) a jump shot fake, a big dribble with the left hand, and a pullup jump shot off the backboard from ten feet away.

3. As player #1 pivots and squares to face the basket, player #2 begins step 1 and then proceeds to execute the five moves in step 2.

4. Each player rebounds his own shot, moves to the opposite lane, and repeats the drill from the opposite side of the court.

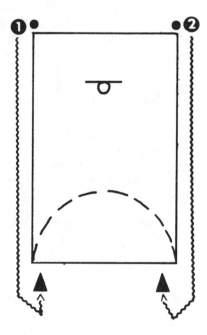

*Figure 119–1*

Coach Will Rey
University of Evansville
Evansville, Indiana

# 120. One-on-One Cone Drill Number Two

**Preparation:** Cones are placed just inside the free throw circle sixteen feet from the baseline. Player #1 and player #2 stand at the points where the lane lines meet the baseline. Each player has a ball.

1. Player #1 begins with a strongside or crossover move and dribbles to the inside of the cones. Once he is past the cone, he jump stops and pivots on his right foot and squares to the basket.

2. At this point player #1 executes five moves: 1) a jab step and a jump shot, 2) a jump shot fake, a strong side move, one dribble with the right hand across face of basket, and a layup on the right side, 3) a jump shot fake, a crossover move, one dribble with the left hand, and a layup on the left side, 4) a jump shot fake, one big dribble with the right hand, and a pullup jump shot from the dotted line, and 5) a jump shot fake, one big dribble with the right hand, and a pullup jump shot off the backboard from ten feet away.

3. As player #1 pivots and squares to the basket, player #2 begins step 1 and then proceeds to execute the five moves in step 2.

4. Each player rebounds his own shots, moves to the opposite lane, and repeats the drill from the opposite side of the court.

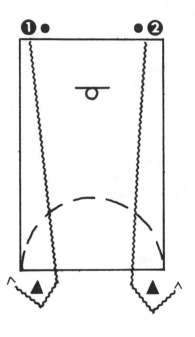

*Figure 120–1*

Coach Will Rey
University of Evansville
Evansville, Indiana

# 121. One-on-One Cone Drill Number Three

**Preparation:** Two cones are placed in the foul line extended area approximately seventeen feet from the basket. Player #1 and player #2 stand at the points where the lane lines meet the baseline. Each player has a ball.

1. Player #1 begins by executing a proper strong side or crossover start and dribbles with his right hand from the baseline to the outside of the cone. Once he is past the cone, he jump stops and pivots on his left foot to square to the basket.

2. At this point player #1 executes five moves from the foul line extended area: 1) a jab step and a jump shot, 2) a jump shot fake, a strong side move, one dribble with the right hand across the face of the basket, and a layup on the right side, 3) a jump shot fake, a crossover move, one dribble with the left hand, and a layup from the left side, 4) a jump shot fake, a big dribble with the right hand, and a pullup jump shot from the dotted line, 5) a jump shot fake, a big dribble with the left hand, and a pullup jump shot off the backboard from ten feet away.

3. As player #1 pivots and squares to face the basket, player #2 begins step 1, and then proceeds to execute the five moves in step 2.

4. Each player rebounds his own shot, moves to the opposite lane, and repeats steps 1-3.

5. Each player repeats the drill, this time moving to the inside of the cones.

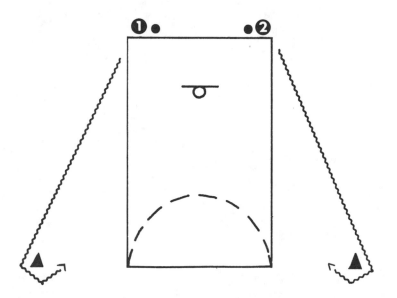

*Figure 121-1*

Coach Will Rey
University of Evansville
Evansville, Indiana

# 122. One-on-One Cone Drill Number Four

**Preparation:** Two cones are placed at the edge of the center jump circle. Player #1 and player #2 stand at the points where the lane lines meet the baseline. Each player has a ball.

1. Player #1 executes a proper start, speed dribbles out to a cone, jump stops, pivots, and squares to the basket.

2. Player #1 must get to the basket in two dribbles. He may utilize an inside or an outside dribble, enabling him to work on different starts.

3. As player #1 pivots and squares to the basket, player #2 begins steps 1 and 2.

4. Each player rebounds his own shot, moves to the opposite lane, and repeats the drill.

**Points of Emphasis:**

- This drill is designed to teach the fundamentals of getting to the basket quickly.

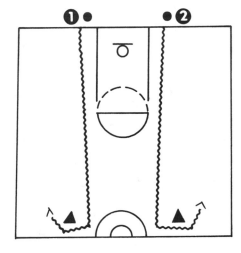

*Figure 122–1*

Coach Will Rey
University of Evansville
Evansville, Indiana

# 123. One-on-One Cone Drill Number Five

**Preparation:** Two cones are placed just inside the free throw circle sixteen feet from the baseline. Player #1 and player #2 stand out of bounds in the foul line extended area. Player #1 and player #2 each have a ball.

1. Player #1 dribbles to the cones on a two-dribble move.

2. He jump stops, squares up to the basket, and shoots a seventeen-foot jump shot.

3. Player #2 executes steps 1 and 2, using a different start than player #1.

4. Each player rebounds his own shot, moves to the opposite lane, and repeats the drill from the opposite side of the court.

**Points of Emphasis:**

– This drill is designed to teach players how to shoot a jump shot off a dribble properly.

*Figure 123–1*

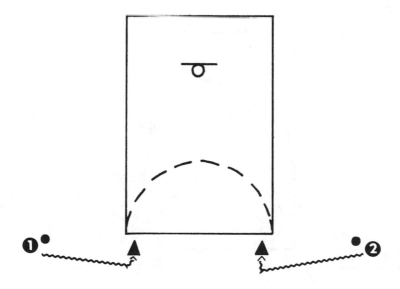

Coach Will Rey
University of Evansville
Evansville, Indiana

# 124. One-on-One Cone Drill Number Six

**Preparation:** Two cones are placed just inside the free throw circle sixteen feet from the baseline. Player #1 and player #2 each have a ball and start out of bounds in the foul line extended area.

1. Player #1 dribbles to the cones on a two-dribble move.

2. He now uses a change of direction move (i.e., behind the back or spin) at the cone and finishes with a one-dribble scoring move to the basket.

3. Player #2 executes steps 1 and 2, using a different start than player #1.

4. Each player rebounds his own shot, moves to the opposite lane, and repeats the drill from the opposite side of the court.

**Points of Emphasis:**

– This drill is designed to teach each player to score off a change of direction move.

*Figure 124–1*

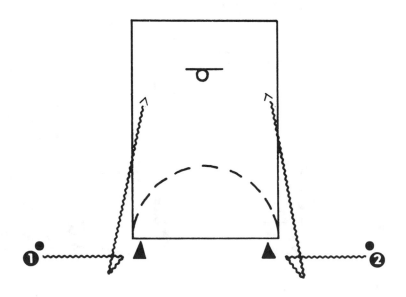

# Mike Fratello
*Atlanta Hawks*

To try to explain what an alligator is, apart from one you'll find in a swamp, is an exercise in futility in the limited space allowed. Suffice it to say that Mike Fratello is the one and only "Five-Star Gator," a nickname pinned on him by tardy campers who frolicked in his "pit." Were Fratello's "pit-bit," implanted during his head coaching reign from 1977–1979, his only contribution to Five-Star, he would still be remembered. But there is a massive file of teaching and coaching information and, above all, a little thing called loyalty that he has also disseminated.

One of the early lessons he taught us is that a coach's height is about as important as the size of his bank account. The NBA learned this years later! Hubie Brown, Fratello's first mentor, brought him to Five-Star in 1969 and slowly but surely the diminutive Fratello, who was learning the ropes under the popular Jimmy Kay at Hackensack High School, developed his own flamboyant style, a cameraman's joy. The former baseball-football letterman at Montclair State was beginning to tower over his peers on the hardwood. He was selected by Rhode Island's Tom Carmody to be his grad assistant, and was chosen by James Madison's Lou Campanelli to "c'mon down" to Harrisonburg, Virginia. Rollie Massimino then picked him to be his top lieutenant at Villanova. Finally, Hubie Brown gave him the big push—twice! He took Michael with him to Atlanta in 1978 and to New York in 1982, and made him the highest-paid assistant coach in NBA history with the Knicks.

But Fratello's most important decision was to remain in Atlanta under Kevin Loughery during Brown's hiatus in 1981. It was Fratello's pivotal year. That non-move set the stage for "Gator's" hiring as head coach of the Hawks in 1983. Blending something old, something new, some things borrowed, and a lot of Dominique, the Hawks clawed their way toward the top of the Central Division again. They soared to the playoffs in 1985–1986 as Fratello was named Coach of the Year and broke a club record in 1986–1987, winning fifty-eight games en route to the Central Division title. Fratello's leadership, personality, and knack for making gutty decisions were the keys to success. But perhaps Fratello's greatest trait of all is his loyalty. Long after Five-Star Camp can do him any good, he returns at least once each summer to address appreciative campers. Mike Fratello doesn't burn his bridges, and he's always building new ones.

*"Good things come in small packages": Mike Fratello and Calvin Murphy at Five-Star's Rosemont site in 1971. Murphy, then a Houston Rocket rookie, is inch-for-inch, pound-for-pound, and shot-for-shot the greatest high school player of all time!*

Coach Mike Fratello
Atlanta Hawks
Atlanta, Georgia

# 125. Defensive Slides Drill

This won't go down with the invention of the steamboat, but Mike Fratello has dreamed up a way to make playing defense fun. The three "Block Drills" are designed to teach various defensive fundamentals in a competitive environment. Done correctly, these drills develop speed and quickness as well as technique. You'll get tired because they encourage hard work. So have competitions with a teammate, but practice first. The Gatorade will taste good. No pun intended, Mike.

**Preparation:** Player stands in the lane and holds a block. Blocks are also placed on each box on the lane (Figure 125-1).

1.  Player gets down in a defensive stance.

2.  Player slides to his left, puts his block down, and picks up the block from the left box.

3.  Player immediately changes direction and goes to the right box, puts his block down, and picks up the block from the right box (Figures 125-2 and 125-3).

4.  Player repeats steps 2-3 for thirty seconds.

**Points of Emphasis:**

- The player should work on quickness, maintaining a good defensive stance, and getting low when playing defense.

- The player must always place the block on the floor rather than throwing or dropping it.

- The drill can also be performed in a competitive situation between two players, with one player on the baseline and another player on the foul line.

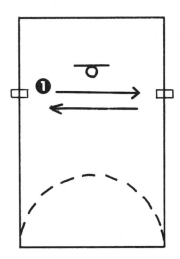

*Figure 125-1*

*Figure* 125–2

*Figure* 125–3

Coach Mike Fratello
Atlanta Hawks
Atlanta, Georgia

# 126. Drop Step Drill

**Preparation:** Blocks are placed at the left box, the right box, and at the top of the key. The player holds another block in his hand. Player stands at the low right box.

1. Player stands in a defensive stance with his right foot forward.

2. Player slides to the top of the key, puts his block down, and picks up the block that is there.

3. Player immediately drop steps and slides to the low left box, puts his block down, and picks up the block that is there.

4. Player slides to the top of the key with his left foot forward, puts his block down, and picks up the block that is there.

5. Player repeats steps 2–4 for thirty seconds.

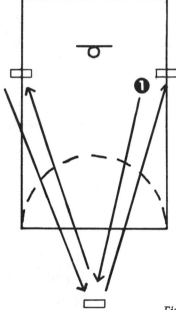

Figure 126–1

**Points of Emphasis:**

– The player should concentrate on working on his upward and downward defensive slides and his drop step.

– The player should work on developing quickness of feet and on keeping low in his stance.

*He never stops teaching: Mike Fratello demonstrates block-out technique. Camper Terry Tyler, second from the right in the background, looks on.*

Coach Mike Fratello
Atlanta Hawks
Atlanta, Georgia

# 127. The Deny Drill

**Preparation:** Blocks are placed at the right box and the foul line extended. The player stands at the right box and holds another block in his right hand.

1. The player slides out as shown in a denial position (Figure 127–1).

2. When the player reaches the foul line extended area, he puts his block down and picks up the block that is there.

3. The player takes two steps in a closed denial position and then either opens up or turns his back to spring to the box to simulate taking away a back-door cut. At the box, the player puts his block down and picks up the block that is there.

4. Player repeats steps 1–3 for thirty seconds.

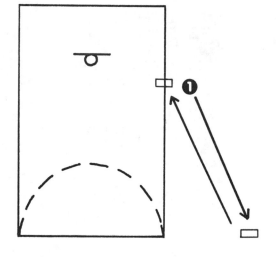

*Figure 127–1*

*Fratello gets around:  Mike Fratello, 1986 NBA Coach of the Year, in Pittsburgh, 1985 (above), and in Honesdale, 1987 (below).*

Jamie Ciampaglio
University of Rhode Island
Kingston, Rhode Island

# Foul Shooting: The Mental Approach

Think back to your season last year. Would your record have been different if you had been able to increase your foul shooting percentage by ten percent? Most coaches believe that forty percent of all close basketball games are decided on the foul line.

I believe that a player's mental approach to foul shooting is extremely important. In my first three years of college I was an eighty to eighty-two percent foul shooter, and I always felt comfortable on the foul line. After my junior season I set up a couple of realistic goals for my senior year. One was to lead the country in foul shooting. To do this, I felt my percentage would have to be in the mid-nineties, so I had to increase my percentage by ten percent.

During the summer before my senior year I listened very closely to all the great shooting coaches at Five-Star. After each conversation I would write down the coaches' main points. The words that came up most frequently were *repetition, concentration, follow-through, eyes on target,* and *practice.*

You must begin by developing good shooting mechanics. Because repetition is one of the most important elements in foul shooting, once you have your mechanics down, you must repeat these movements again and again from the foul line. Come up with a routine that you feel comfortable with and practice it every time you shoot a free throw. My routine consisted of the following: I would bounce the ball three times, and with each bounce I would say, "front rim, concentration, follow-through." By going through this routine and repeating it over and over, I was able to block out all other thoughts. Foul shooting became easier and easier as the months passed, and I felt increasingly confident and comfortable at the foul line.

Concentration is another important element of foul shooting. I am annoyed by foul shooters who celebrate after each foul shot with high fives or by clapping their hands. How many times have you seen a player make the first free throw, celebrate, and then miss the second? I believe one of the reasons for this was that their concentration was broken after the first free throw. So please, save your celebration until after you make both shots.

Once you have your mechanics and your routine down and you feel very comfortable every time you step up to the line, you must practice. To help myself practice, I developed a game I call "Swish City," in which a player must shoot extremely well in order to win. To play the game you take thirty free throws and you receive one point for any made free throw and two points for a swish. You must score forty points to win. After awhile you start to concentrate so hard on swishing every shot that you are not satisfied with simply making a free throw.

By the way, my senior year I did not lead the country in foul shooting, but I did finish in the top five at ninety-one percent.

# Ralph Willard
*Syracuse University*

Despite copping Coach of the Year honors five times in twelve years in the rugged Nassau-Suffolk (Long Island) Catholic High School League, which included now-defunct St. Agnes (Billy Donovan), Holy Trinity (Matt Doherty), and St. Anthony's (Rich Simkus and Tom Hicks), Ralph Willard remains one of the best-kept coaching secrets in the nation. While at St. Dominic's (Oyster Bay) he won four league championships, finished in first place on two occasions in the Long Island playoffs, and brought home the New York State title in 1980. He sent Tim Kempton to Notre Dame and the Clippers and a gaggle of players to mid- and low-major colleges.

After a year as a top aide to Dick Berg at Hofstra University (Hempstead, Long Island), Willard acted as a volunteer assistant to Jim Boeheim at Syracuse in 1986–1987. The egoless Boeheim will be the first to admit that "Coach Ralph's" mental gymnastics with Seikaly, Coleman, and especially Sherman Douglas proved a boon to the Orangemen's heroic NCAA Tourney run.

Ralph's playing career included swinging for Holy Cross and Jack Donahue—remember Power Memorial and Lou Alcindor?—and no doubt he deposited large amounts of learning in his "coaching bank" from that adventure. He's accrued major interest from his fourteen years at Five-Star and is constantly being tested with the toughest station assignments and Staff Day topics. Like he owns "The City Game!" For the purposes of this book we call it "moving or playing without the ball," but let's face it, there was a time when that was "The City Game."

*No, it's not a knockout punch or an old dance step. It's simply the old one-two, an intricate two-step maneuver to get free from pressure taught by station-master Ralph Willard.*

Coach Ralph Willard
Syracuse University
Syracuse, New York

# 128. Two-Step Pop-Out Drill

In these three drills Coach Willard has made a withdrawal from his huge "coaching bank" to teach you three moves that will get you free from pressure. If you are considered a Division I prospect, then undoubtably you're being at least double teamed in high school. Now this might be the most important thing you'll read in this book: Unless you are 7'0'' or "Mugsy" Bogues, *you can't be a factor at the next level without total mastery of these three moves!* If you believe nothing else, believe that! So work diligently on freeing up from overplays, maintain your 20+ points per game average, and someday soon you'll be making sizable deposits—of the real thing—in *your* bank account.

**Preparation:** Player #1 starts at the right foul line extended area. Player #2 stands to the right of the key and player #3 stands at the top of the key. Player #2 is the defensive player and stands in a denial stance. Player #3 has the ball and serves as the passer.

1. Player #1 takes one step down to the basket with his inside (left) foot.

2. Player #1 steps directly into player #2 with his right foot and tries to step between player #2's legs.

3. Player #1 now reverse pivots off his right foot and swings his back and rear end into player #2's thighs, making sure his hands and arms are at shoulder level to seal him off from the passing lane.

4. Player #1 now completes the move by pivoting off his left foot and stepping out away from the defender with his right foot, showing his right hand as a target for player #3 at the same time.

5. Player #3 passes the ball to player #1.

6. Players repeat the drill ten to fifteen times from each side of the basket.

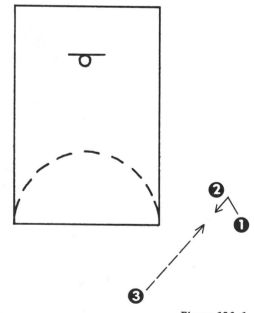

*Figure 128–1*

Coach Ralph Willard
Syracuse University
Syracuse, New York

# 129. Jam Down into Back Door Drill

**Preparation:** Player #1 stands at the left foul line extended area. Player #2 is the defender and stands in a denial stance on the left side of the lane. Player #3 is the offensive player and stands at the top of the key on the left side. Player #3 is in possession of the ball.

1. Player #1 walks player #2 down to the low box.

2. After he reaches the low box, player #1 jams off his inside (left) foot, changes his pace, and aggressively pops out to receive the ball from player #3.

3. Once player #1 shows his hand for the pass, he changes direction by pivoting and pushing off his outside foot.

4. Player #1's first step should be behind the defender (player #2) to seal him off, and player #1 must show a target hand for the passer (player #3).

5. Player #3 throws a bounce pass to player #1, cutting off the back door.

6. Players repeat the drill ten to fifteen times from each side of the basket.

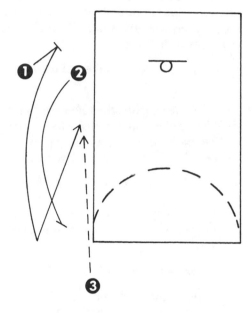

*Figure 129–1*

**Coach Ralph Willard**
**Syracuse University**
**Syracuse, New York**

# 130. Jam Down Drill (V Cut)

**Preparation:** Player #1 stands at the left foul line extended area. Player #2 is the defender and stands in a denial stance on the left side of the lane. Player #3 is the offensive player and stands at the head of the key on the left side. Player #3 is in possession of the ball.

1. Player #1 walks player #2 down to the low box (Figure 130–1).

2. After he reaches the low box, player #1 jams off his inside (left) foot, changes his pace, and aggressively pops out to receive the ball from player #3.

3. As player #1 reaches the foul line extended area, he steps to the passer (player #3) with his inside foot, reaches out, and shows his target hand (Figure 130–2).

4. Player #3 passes the ball to player #1.

5. After player #1 receives the ball, he squares up to the basket and assumes a triple threat position.

6. Players begin one-on-one play.

7. Players repeat the drill ten to fifteen times from each side of the basket.

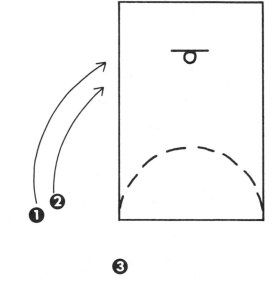

*Figure 130–1*

**Points of Emphasis:**

– Players should concentrate on a different move each day during the one-on-one play.

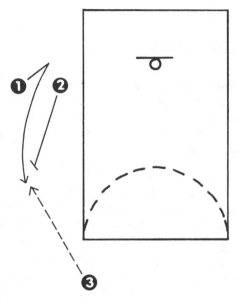

*Figure 130–2*

*A camper waits patiently for Tom McCorry to throw the basketball.*

Ralph Willard
Syracuse University
Syracuse, New York

# Moving Without the Ball

Having a "game" without the ball is a must for any player who wants to advance in basketball. Consider that the average player spends about ninety-five percent of his time during a game without the ball. He must develop skills that will enable him to receive the ball in his most effective scoring area when he wants it, versus the various pressure defenses employed in today's game.

The key elements of moving without the ball are: 1) change of pace, 2) change of direction, 3) pivoting, 4) head and upper body fakes, and 5) proper use of the hands in faking and receiving the ball. Let us look briefly at the importance of each one of these elements in developing an effective "game" without the ball.

1. **Change of Pace:** Any offensive player is quicker than his defensive opponent without the ball for the first two steps after a change of pace. The more dramatic the change, the more open a player is likely to be.

2. **Change of Direction:** A basic rule for getting open without the ball is to avoid going in a straight line to the ball. Each player must learn to play with his knees bent and his body in a good balance to change direction effectively.

3. **Pivoting:** Pivoting and reverse pivoting are skills that must be learned to change direction effectively and to create and maintain offensive position advantages gained by effective movement without the ball. Sealing the defender by pivoting and reverse pivoting is an important finishing move that must be learned.

4. **Head and Upper Body Fakes:** The offensive player should learn to move his head and upper body to simulate a change of direction, thus getting the defender to react and move his feet without having the offensive player move his feet. This always gives the offensive player the advantage and makes him quicker.

5. **Use of Hands in Faking and Receiving:** One of the most effective ways to get the defensive player to over-commit prior to the offensive player's change of direction is for the offensive player to "show his hands in the passing lane." This forces the defender to react to the offensive player's extended arms and hop into the passing lane in order to deny the offensive player the ball. This insures the offensive player effective first steps in his back door move. Receiving the ball effectively is the final objective when moving without the ball, and the player must learn to show a target hand, reach out to catch the ball, and follow the ball all the way into his hands with his eyes by nodding his head down toward his hands as he receives the ball.

All these elements must be practiced repeatedly until they become an instinctive part of the player's "game" without the ball.

# Ed Schilling
*Miami University*

This question may never appear on *Time Out for Trivia,* but Todd Donohue will be happy to learn that only two high school basketball players who averaged under ten points per game were ever selected for a national All-Star game in this country. Who are they, you ask? Well, one was Tyrone "Mugsy" Bogues (Bullets and Wake Forest), who coined more assists than points for Bob Wade's Dunbar Poets; and Ed Schilling, who squeezed out a 9.2 norm while riding shotgun for Lebanon (Indiana) High School in 1983–1984.

"The Chill" started in Max Rein's last hoop extravaganza, the Kosair Classic in Rupp Arena, and went on to set every assist record in Miami of Ohio history (including a single game mark of seventeen), ending his college career with 640 aids, third all-time in the MAC.

Ed's father was a record-breaking NAIA coach at Marion (Indiana) College, and it's evident the coaching-teaching genes have been passed from father to son. Also his work ethic! Schilling rates with Rumeal Robinson (Michigan) as one of the hardest-working campers in Five-Star history. As a four-year counselor, he's one of the few undergraduates to man an NBA station, the "Chill Drill" being the end result of his overachievements.

Ed Schilling
Miami University
Oxford, Ohio

# 131. The Chill Drill

As you begin this drill, keep in mind that Rome wasn't built in a day—start slowly and increase your speed with practice. Once you are able to perform this drill consistently at top speed, with both hands, nobody will be able to take the ball away from you.

**Preparation:** Player stands at the left side of the court where the baseline and sideline intersect. He holds the ball in his right hand.

1. Player executes an inside-out move. To do this, he dribbles twice on the line directly in front of him. On the third dribble, he takes the ball across his body and bounces it to the left of the line in front of his left foot. Then he explodes past an imaginary defender by pushing off his left foot and pushing the ball in front of him back on the line, trying to cover as much ground as possible. Player must keep his knees bent and keep his body on the line, moving only the ball. He should end at position A (Figure 131–1). Note that the ball remains in player's right hand during this step.

2. Player repeats step 1 from position B.

3. Player comes to a quick jump stop where the sideline and half court line intersect (position C). He executes a reverse or spin dribble, keeping his left foot on the ground and making sure to reach (hook) with his right leg in order to beat the defender. Player pulls the ball as he gets the imaginary defender on his back, then switches the ball to his left hand and dribbles quickly to position D.

4. At position D, player should pull the ball back beside his left knee as he executes two low, quick retreat dribbles until he reaches position E. This retreat step helps create space against a trap or double team.

5. At position E, player executes a quick, low crossover dribble, switching the ball to his right hand.

6. Player takes two dribbles and comes to a quick jump stop at position F. He executes a half-a-spin move, which is the counter move to the reverse or spin dribble. He does this by pivoting 180 degrees on his left foot and pulling the ball until it is directly in front of his right foot. Then he bounces the ball with force in front of his right foot when his back is to the defender. Next he explodes out by pivoting on his left foot.

7. Player plants his right foot where the sideline and half court line intersect (position G) and executes a behind-the-back dribble from his right hand to his left hand, trying to cover as much ground as possible by pushing off his right foot toward position H.

8. Player then executes a stutter-step to freeze the defender and makes a quick, low crossover, switching the ball from his left to his right hand.

9. Player then makes one hard dribble to the basket for a layup with his right hand.

**Points of Emphasis:**

- As the player pulls the ball in step 3, he must be careful not to palm it.    He should keep his hand on top of the ball.

- Every move is made with the intention of beating and going by the defender.

- The drill should also be performed beginning on the right side of the court, starting with the ball in the left hand, so that moves can be perfected with either hand.

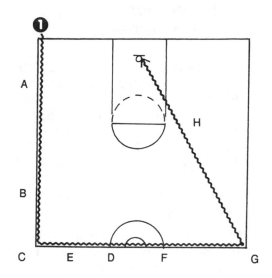

*Figure 131–1*

*A Five-Star camper performing the "Chill Drill."*

# Buddy Gardler
*Cardinal O'Hara High School*

The late Will Rogers once said, "I never met a man I didn't like." Buddy Gardler's acerbic wit has caused more than one of his targets to retort, "Yeah, but he never met Buddy Gardler!" Actually, "Mr. Warmth," as he is lovingly called by his Five-Star compatriots, is one of the most popular figures on the staff and has been for the past eighteen years. The "dean" of Five-Star resident coaches played his first two years of college ball at St. Joe's under Jack Ramsey and the last two sticking his lefty jumper for Jack McKinney. It's hard to imagine a more fertile training ground for a budding coach. And the future was now. Late in his senior year in college, Gardler was named head coach of Bishop Kenrick High School in Norristown, Pennsylvania, unusual even for those days.

He went 98–56 at Kenrick and was twice named Montgomery County Coach of the Year. He tried the college scene for a year with Jimmy Lynam at American University, but his heart was in high school. So it was back to the Catholic League of Philly. In eleven years at Cardinal O'Hara in Springfield, Coach Gardler has compiled a remarkable 160–78 log that includes a Delaware County 1980 Coach of the Year accolade and a Final Four berth in two of the last three years.

In 1980 he was chosen to coach in Sonny Vaccaro's prestigious Dapper Dan Roundball Classic in Pittsburgh. He followed that up with a stint for Max Rein in the 1982 Derby Classic in Louisville and handled the East squad in the 1983 McDonald's All-American game in the Omni in Atlanta for Bob Geoghan. His lectures, stations, and special closing-day seminars on shooting at Five-Star are almost works of art.

*An overflow crowd of guards greets Buddy Gardler at one of his many Staff Day lectures.*

Buddy Gardler
Cardinal O'Hara High School
Springfield, Pennsylvania

# The Mental Approach to Shooting

Coach Gardler can still fill it up with the best of them but here the "Shot Doctor" dissects the mental aspects of shooting, placing special emphasis on the twenty-one-foot three-point play. As you can read, he's operating in rare form.

## Shooting — Points to Remember

1. Shooting is the easiest and most enjoyable skill to improve—all that is needed is a ball and a basket.

2. Concentration is most important.

3. Average shooters get minutes, good shooters become franchises, and great shooters receive pro contracts.

4. A player of any age can correct his shot. It's a matter of putting in hours—the more hours, the more confidence. Concentration is most important.

5. I've seen players with awful form who can make a shot because they have worked on that shot and believe they will make it. They too can improve (for example, go from forty-five to fifty percent). Think of the many players who made it to the pros based on their athletic ability and then worked hard on their shot to keep themselves in the pros.

6. In nineteen years of coaching I feel that most high school players think shooting skills come too easily. The main things to correct are often the easiest things to correct—working on them is the hard part.

7. It is important to practice correct shooting form, which includes:
   - *Hand position:* Fingers are spread, with the index finger placed in the middle of the ball. The guide-hand thumb forms a T with the shooting-hand thumb.
   - *Follow-through:* The most common mistake slow players make is to rush the follow-through.
   - *Feet:* Players should spot up and get their feet under the shot. Quicker players usually have a tendency to float on the shot.

## Shooting Practice — In-season and Out-of-season

Most of our in-season and out-of-season work centers on freeing up for the jump shot. All of our shooting work starts at a slow pace and becomes faster. We then finish by practicing foul shots.

1. When someone is stale or is in a slump, he practices a lot of one-handed shooting. If you can't shoot with one hand, you can't shoot.

2. Players do a lot of spot shooting with no defense, including:

- shooting backward, starting in close and moving out.
- shooting forward, starting in close and moving out, aiming for a spot on the backboard. The farther out the palyer is, the higher the spot he aims for.
- shooting from the perimeter areas, both standing still and jumpers. Make three and move.

3. One game we play is taps. A player tries to make twenty-one baskets in a row from the three-point line. If he misses and another player tips it in, the first player goes out and the other player goes in. (Play for sodas—it puts pressure on.)

4. All of our one-on-one games start at the three-point line. A three-pointer counts for two, and a made shot inside counts for one. We limit the number of dribbles the offense has to three.

## Shooting Practice—In-season

Our in-season shooting work focuses on shooting against defense—first passive, and then hard defense. Practice sessions include the following two drills.

1. The defensive player throws out to a player on the three-point line, and then defense flies at the player. If the offensive player can get off a shot, he should. If the offensive player cannot get off a shot, he should throw fake and use one dribble to spot up.

2. Gradually turn this into a controlled situation where the offense still uses one dribble to get a shot. Make it as similar to game conditions as possible—that's the only way to improve the fake and the shot. Remember, good shooters need a ball fake or a foot fake to free themselves.

## Shooting Practice—Off-season

The off-season is the best time to work on your shot. Shooting sessions should be about forty minutes long, the same as your classes, which is about how long you can give peak concentration. Don't expect miracles—shooting improves gradually. But the more hours you put in, the more you'll believe in your shot!

Herb Sendek
Providence College
Providence, Rhode Island

# Academics By Sendek

With Proposition 48 in the wings in 1985, we "commissioned" Coach Sendek to devise an academic lecture for Five-Star's younger campers. It was such a rousing success that "Academics by Sendek" is now offered to young and old alike, whenever the "Providence Prodigy" can attend. It almost makes us want to go back to school and do it right!

## Keys to Becoming a Better Student

1. Study so much and so hard that even angels can do no more.
2. Sit in the front of the class toward the middle.
3. Give the teacher your undivided attention.
4. Develop an organized and efficient system of note taking.
5. Ask at least one question per class period.
6. Stay after class and make appointments to see your teachers for individual help.
7. Try to respond intelligently to questions asked in class.
8. Never miss or be late for class.
9. Always use good manners.
10. Work to learn each and every day.
11. Be extremely organized.
12. Use time wisely.
13. Develop the ability to concentrate.
14. Do more than is expected.
15. As you study, write down any questions you may have.
16. Develop the ability to reason but rely on the power of memory.
17. Read! Read! Read! Read! Read!
18. Eliminate excuses and expectations of favors.
19. Dare to stand alone!
20. Seek outside help.

## Keys to Organization

1. Keep a separate, clearly marked notebook and folder for each class.

2. Date your papers, number the pages, and put your name on them.

3. Keep a fixed place for frequently used reference materials and return them after use.*

4. Write down all assignments on one piece of paper and keep it in a specific, easily accessible, and frequently looked at place. Check off assignments as they are completed.

5. Underline or highlight in books with a color-coded system.

6. If you cannot complete a task in one session, divide it into subparts which can be completed in one session.*

7. When you finish a work session on a given subject, plan what to do next when you return to that subject. Leave a note as a reminder.*

8. Be neat. Use a ruler and compass and write legibly.

## Keys to Using Time Wisely

1. Establish a fixed schedule, taking into account difficulty of subject and relative importance.*

2. Study a subject as closely as possible to the lecture on that subject.*

3. Schedule subjects that require a great deal of concentration for times when you are most alert.*

4. The schedule should include a weekly review and planning session.*

5. Follow your schedule closely but remain flexible.

## Keys to Concentration

1. Work in silence.

2. Use your work space only for work.*

3. Schedule short rests away from your work space.*

4. After solving a problem, review the difficulty and the way in which you overcame it.*

5. Avoid daydreaming. Mentally summarize each paragraph as you study. Use a timer to help schedule study sessions.*

Your success in school and in life has a great deal to do with the decisions you make. Many of these decisions have nothing to do with IQ, but instead test your self-discipline and courage.

[The points denoted by asterisks were taken from *The Complete Problem Solver* by John R. Hayes (Philadelphia: The Franklin Institute Press, 1981, pp. 239–242). The points not denoted by asterisks are explained in *Proposition 100: Education for Life* by Bill Shay and Herb Sendek.]

*You never know who's going to show:  Above, Jim Paxson (Chicago Bulls) displays NBA form as a surprise guest clinician at Station 13, while Detroit Piston assistant Ron Rothstein draws another big crowd, below.*

*Insert the numbers of the drills you have practiced into the corresponding spaces below.*

|  | SUN. | MON. | TUES. | WED. | THURS. | FRI. | SAT. |
|---|---|---|---|---|---|---|---|
| CONDITIONING DRILLS |  |  |  |  |  |  |  |
| BALLHANDLING/ DRIBBLING DRILLS |  |  |  |  |  |  |  |
| PASSING DRILLS |  |  |  |  |  |  |  |
| ONE-ON-ONE MOVES |  |  |  |  |  |  |  |
| SHOOTING DRILLS |  |  |  |  |  |  |  |
| REBOUNDING DRILLS |  |  |  |  |  |  |  |
| DEFENSE DRILLS |  |  |  |  |  |  |  |
| BIG MAN DEVELOPMENT DRILLS |  |  |  |  |  |  |  |
| BASKETBALL SMORGASBORD |  |  |  |  |  |  |  |

*Insert the numbers of the drills you have practiced into the corresponding spaces below.*

|  | SUN. | MON. | TUES. | WED. | THURS. | FRI. | SAT. |
|---|---|---|---|---|---|---|---|
| CONDITIONING DRILLS |  |  |  |  |  |  |  |
| BALLHANDLING/ DRIBBLING DRILLS |  |  |  |  |  |  |  |
| PASSING DRILLS |  |  |  |  |  |  |  |
| ONE-ON-ONE MOVES |  |  |  |  |  |  |  |
| SHOOTING DRILLS |  |  |  |  |  |  |  |
| REBOUNDING DRILLS |  |  |  |  |  |  |  |
| DEFENSE DRILLS |  |  |  |  |  |  |  |
| BIG MAN DEVELOPMENT DRILLS |  |  |  |  |  |  |  |
| BASKETBALL SMORGASBORD |  |  |  |  |  |  |  |

*Insert the numbers of the drills you have practiced into the corresponding spaces below.*

| | SUN. | MON. | TUES. | WED. | THURS. | FRI. | SAT. |
|---|---|---|---|---|---|---|---|
| CONDITIONING DRILLS | | | | | | | |
| BALLHANDLING/ DRIBBLING DRILLS | | | | | | | |
| PASSING DRILLS | | | | | | | |
| ONE-ON-ONE MOVES | | | | | | | |
| SHOOTING DRILLS | | | | | | | |
| REBOUNDING DRILLS | | | | | | | |
| DEFENSE DRILLS | | | | | | | |
| BIG MAN DEVELOPMENT DRILLS | | | | | | | |
| BASKETBALL SMORGASBORD | | | | | | | |

*Insert the numbers of the drills you have practiced into the corresponding spaces below.*

|  | SUN. | MON. | TUES. | WED. | THURS. | FRI. | SAT. |
|---|---|---|---|---|---|---|---|
| CONDITIONING DRILLS |  |  |  |  |  |  |  |
| BALLHANDLING/ DRIBBLING DRILLS |  |  |  |  |  |  |  |
| PASSING DRILLS |  |  |  |  |  |  |  |
| ONE-ON-ONE MOVES |  |  |  |  |  |  |  |
| SHOOTING DRILLS |  |  |  |  |  |  |  |
| REBOUNDING DRILLS |  |  |  |  |  |  |  |
| DEFENSE DRILLS |  |  |  |  |  |  |  |
| BIG MAN DEVELOPMENT DRILLS |  |  |  |  |  |  |  |
| BASKETBALL SMORGASBORD |  |  |  |  |  |  |  |